WORD
PROBLEMS

GRE Math Strategy Guide

The Word Problems guide educates students in the art of translating challenging word problems into organized data, as well as providing structured frameworks for attacking each question type.

Word Problems GRE Strategy Guide, Second Edition

10-digit International Standard Book Number: 1-935707-54-X
13-digit International Standard Book Number: 978-1-935707-54-7
eISBN: 978-0-981853-39-0

Copyright © 2011 MG Prep, Inc.

ALL RIGHTS RESERVED. No part of this work may be reproduced or used in any form or by any means—graphic, electronic, or mechanical, including photocopying, recording, taping, Web distribution—without the prior written permission of the publisher, MG Prep Inc.

Note: *GRE, Graduate Record Examination, Educational Testing Services,* and *ETS* are all registered trademarks of Educational Testing Services, which neither sponsors nor is affiliated in any way with this product.

8 GUIDE INSTRUCTIONAL SERIES

Math GRE Preparation Guides

Algebra
(ISBN: 978–1–935707–47–9)

Fractions, Decimals, & Percents
(ISBN: 978–1–935707–48–6)

Geometry
(ISBN: 978–1–935707–49–3)

Number Properties
(ISBN: 978–1–935707–50–9)

Word Problems
(ISBN: 978–1–935707–54–7)

Quantitative Comparisons & Data Interpretation
(ISBN: 978–1–935707–51–6)

Verbal GRE Preparation Guides

Reading Comprehension & Essays
(ISBN: 978–1–935707–52–3)

Text Completion & Sentence Equivalence
(ISBN: 978–1–935707–53–0)

*Manhattan*GRE

March 15th, 2011

Dear Student,

Thank you for picking up one of the Manhattan GRE Strategy Guides—we hope that it ends up being just what you need to prepare for the new GRE.

As with most accomplishments, there were many people involved in the book that you're holding. First and foremost is Zeke Vanderhoek, the founder of MG Prep. Zeke was a lone tutor in New York when he started the Company in 2000. Now, ten years later, the Company has Instructors and offices nationwide and contributes to the studies and successes of thousands of students each year.

Our Manhattan GRE Strategy Guides are based on the continuing experiences of our Instructors and our students. On the Company side, we are indebted to many of our Instructors, including but not limited to Roman Altshuler, Chris Berman, Faruk Bursal, Jen Dziura, Dmitry Farber, Stacey Koprince, David Mahler, Seb Moosapoor, Stephanie Moyerman, Chris Ryan, Michael Schwartz, Tate Shafer, Emily Sledge, Tommy Wallach, and Ryan Wessel, all of whom either wrote or edited the books to their present form. Dan McNaney and Cathy Huang provided their formatting expertise to make the books as user-friendly as possible. Last, many people, too numerous to list here but no less appreciated, assisted in the development of the online resources that accompany this guide.

At Manhattan GRE, we continually aspire to provide the best Instructors and resources possible. We hope that you'll find our dedication manifest in this book. If you have any comments or questions, please e-mail me at dan@manhattangre.com. I'll be sure that your comments reach our curriculum team—and I'll read them too.

Best of luck in preparing for the GRE!

Sincerely,

Dan

Dan Gonzalez
Managing Director
Manhattan GRE

HOW TO ACCESS YOUR ONLINE STUDENT CENTER

If you…

⊙ ## are a registered Manhattan GRE student

and have received this book as part of your course materials, you have AUTOMATIC access to ALL of our online resources. To access these resources, follow the instructions in the Welcome Guide provided to you at the start of your program. Do NOT follow the instructions below.

⊙ ## purchased this book from the Manhattan GRE Online store
or at one of our Centers

1. Go to: http://www.manhattangre.com/studentcenter.cfm

2. Log in using the username and password used when your account was set up. Your one year of online access begins on the day that you purchase the book from the Manhattan GRE online store or at one of our centers.

⊙ ## purchased this book at a retail location

1. Go to: http://www.manhattangre.com/access.cfm

2. Log in or create an account.

3. Follow the instructions on the screen.

Your one year of online access begins on the day that you register your book at the above URL.

You only need to register your product ONCE at the above URL. To use your online resources any time AFTER you have completed the registration process, login to the following URL: http://www.manhattangre.com/studentcenter.cfm

Please note that online access is non-transferable. This means that only NEW and UNREGISTERED copies of the book will grant you online access. Previously used books will not provide any online resources.

⊙ ## purchased an e-book version of this book

1. Create an account with Manhattan GRE at the website: https://www.manhattangre.com/createaccount.cfm

2. Email a copy of your purchase receipt to books@manhattangre.com to activate your resources. Please be sure to use the same email address to create an account that you used to purchase the e-book.

For any technical issues, email books@manhattangre.com or call 646-254-6479.

TABLE OF CONTENTS

g

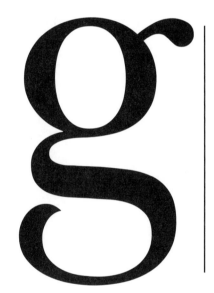

Chapter 1

of

WORD PROBLEMS

INTRODUCTION &
THE REVISED GRE

In This Chapter . . .

- Introduction, and How to Use Manhattan GRE's Strategy Guides
- The Revised GRE
- Question Formats in Detail

Introduction, and How to Use Manhattan GRE's Strategy Guides

We know that you're looking to succeed on the GRE so that you can go to graduate school and do the things you want to do in life.

We also know that you might not have done math since high school, and that you may never have learned words like "adumbrate" or "sangfroid." We know that it's going to take hard work on your part to get a top GRE score, and that's why we've put together the only set of books that will take you from the basics all the way up to the material you need to master for a near-perfect score, or whatever your score goal may be. You've taken the first step. Now it's time to get to work!

How to Use These Materials

Manhattan GRE's materials are comprehensive. But keep in mind that, depending on your score goal, it may not be necessary to "get" absolutely everything. Grad schools only see your overall Quantitative, Verbal, and Writing scores—they don't see exactly which strengths and weaknesses went into creating those scores.

You may be enrolled in one of our courses, in which case you already have a syllabus telling you in what order you should approach the books. But if you bought this book online or at a bookstore, feel free to approach the books—and even the chapters within the books—in whatever order works best for you. *For the most part, the books, and the chapters within them, are independent; you don't have to master one section before moving on to the next.* So if you're having a hard time with something in particular, you can make a note to come back to it later and move on to another section. Similarly, it may not be necessary to solve every single practice problem for every section. As you go through the material, continually assess whether you understand and can apply the principles in each individual section and chapter. The best way to do this is to solve the Check Your Skills and Practice Problems throughout. If you're confident you have a concept or method down, feel free to move on. If you struggle with something, make note of it for further review. Stay active in your learning and oriented toward the test—it's easy to read something and think you understand it, only to have trouble applying it in the 1–2 minutes you have to solve a problem.

Study Skills

As you're studying for the GRE, try to integrate your learning into your everyday life. For example, vocabulary is a big part of the GRE, as well as something you just can't "cram" for—you're going to want to do at least a little bit of vocab every day. So, try to learn and internalize a little bit at a time, switching up topics often to help keep things interesting.

Keep in mind that, while many of your study materials are on paper (including ETS's most recent source of official GRE questions, *The Official Guide to the GRE revised General Test*), your exam will be administered on a computer. Because this is a computer-based test, you will NOT be able to underline portions of reading passages, write on diagrams of geometry figures, or otherwise physically mark up problems. So get used to this now. Solve the problems in these books on scratch paper. (Each of our books talks specifically about what to write down for different problem types).

Again, as you study stay focused on the test-day experience. As you progress, work on timed drills and sets of questions. Eventually, you should be taking full practice tests (available at **www.manhattangre.com**) under actual timed conditions.

The Revised GRE

As of August 1, 2011, the Quantitative and Verbal sections of the GRE will undergo a number of changes. The actual body of knowledge being tested won't change, but the *way* it is tested will. Here's a brief summary of what to expect, followed by a more comprehensive assessment of the new exam.

Overall, the general format of the test will change. The length of the test will increase from about 3.5 hours to about 4 hours. There will be two scored math sections and two scored verbal sections rather than one of each, and a new score scale of 130–170 will be used in place of the old 200–800 scale. More on this later.

The Verbal section of the GRE will change dramatically. The Analogies and Antonym questions will disappear. The Sentence Completions and Reading Comprehension will remain, to be expanded and remixed in a few new ways. Vocabulary will still be important, but only in the context of complete sentences. That is, you'll no longer have to worry about vocabulary words standing alone. So for those who dislike learning vocabulary words, the changes will provide partial relief. For those who were looking forward to getting lots of points just for memorizing words, the Manhattan GRE verbal strategy guides will prepare you for the shift.

The Quant section of the GRE prior to August 1, 2011 is composed of multiple choice problems, Quantitative Comparisons, and Data Interpretation questions (which are really a subset of multiple choice problems). The revised test will contain two new problem formats in addition to the current problem formats. However, the type of math, and the difficulty of the math, will remain unchanged.

Additionally, a small four-function calculator with a square root button will appear on-screen. Many test takers will rejoice at the advent of this calculator! It is true that the GRE calculator will reduce emphasis on computation—but look out for problems, such as percents questions with tricky wording, that are likely to foil those who rely on the calculator too much. *In short, the calculator may make your life a bit easier from time to time, but you will never <u>need</u> the calculator to solve a problem.*

Finally, don't worry about whether these new problem types are "harder" or "easier." You are being judged against other test takers, all of whom are in the same boat. So if the new formats are harder, they are harder for other test takers as well.

EXAM STRUCTURE

The revised test has six sections. You will get a ten-minute break between the third and fourth sections and a one-minute break between the others. The Analytical Writing section is always first. The other five sections can be seen in any order and will include:

- Two Verbal Reasoning sections (approximately 20 questions each in exactly 30 minutes per section)

- Two Quantitative Reasoning sections (approximately 20 questions each in exactly 35 minutes per section)

- Either an "unscored" section or a "research" section

An unscored section will look just like a third Verbal or Quantitative Reasoning section, and you will <u>not</u> be told which of them doesn't count. If you get a research section, it will be identified as such.

Section Type	# Questions	Time	Scored?
Analytical Writing	2 essays	30 minutes each	Yes
Verbal #1	Approx. 20	30 minutes	Yes
Quantitative #1	Approx. 20	35 minutes	Yes
Verbal #2	Approx. 20	30 minutes	Yes
Quantitative #2	Approx. 20	35 minutes	Yes
Unscored Section (verbal or quant)	Approx. 20	30 or 35 min	No
Research Section	Varies	Varies	No

10 min break

one or the other, but not both

Later in the chapter, we'll look at all the question formats in detail.

USING THE CALCULATOR

The addition of a small, four-function calculator with a square root button means that those taking the revised test can forget re-memorizing their times tables or square roots. However, the calculator is not a cure-all; in many problems, the difficulty is in figuring out what numbers to put into the calculator in the first place. In some cases, using a calculator will actually be less helpful than doing the problem some other way. Let's look at an example:

If x is the remainder when (11)(7) is divided by 4 and y is the remainder when (14)(6) is divided by 13, what is the value of $x + y$?

Solution: This problem is designed so that the calculator won't tell the whole story. Certainly the calculator will tell us that $11 \times 7 = 77$. When you divide 77 by 4, however, the calculator yields an answer of 19.25. The remainder is *not* 0.25 (a remainder is always a whole number).

You might just go back to your pencil and paper, and find the largest multiple of 4 that is less than 77. Since 4 DOES go into 76, we can conclude that 4 would leave a remainder of 1 when dividing into 77. (Notice that we don't even need to know how many times 4 goes into 76, just that it goes in. One way to mentally "jump" to 76 is to say, *4 goes into 40, so it goes into 80 … that's a bit too big, so take away 4 to get 76.*) You could also multiply the leftover 0.25 times 4 (the divisor) to find the remainder of 1.

However, it is also possible to use the calculator to find a remainder. Divide 77 by 4 to get 19.25. Thus, 4 goes into 77 nineteen times, with a remainder left over. Now use your calculator to multiply 19 (JUST 19, not 19.25) by 4. You will get 76. The remainder is $77 - 76 = 1$. Therefore, $x = 1$.

Use the same technique to find y. Multiply 14×6 to get 84. Divide 84 by 13 to get 6.46… Ignore everything after the decimal, and just multiply 6 by 13 to get 78. The remainder is therefore $84 - 78 = 6$. Therefore, $y = 6$.

Since we are looking for $x + y$ and $1 + 6 = 7$, the answer is 7.

You can see that blind faith in the calculator can be dangerous. Use it responsibly! And this leads us to…

PRACTICE USING THE CALCULATOR!

On the new GRE, the on-screen calculator will slow you down or lead to incorrect answers if you're not careful! If you plan to use the thing on test day (which you should), you'll want to pactice first.

We have created an online practice calculator for your use. To access this calculator, go to www.manhattangre.com and sign in to the student center using the instructions on the "How to Access Your Online Student Center" page found at the front of this book.

In addition to the calculator, you will see instructions for how to use the calculator. Be sure to read these

instructions and work through the associated exercises. Throughout our math books, you will see the

symbol. This symbol means "use the calculator here!" As much as possible, have the online practice calculator up

and running during your review of our math books. You'll have the chance to use the on-screen calculator when

you take our practice exams as well.

Navigating the Questions in a Section

Another change for test takers on the new GRE is the ability to move freely around the questions in a section… you can go forward and backward one-by-one and can even jump directly to any question from the "review list." The review list provides a snapshot of which questions you have answered, which ones you have tagged for "mark and review," and which are incomplete, either because you didn't select enough answers or because you selected too many (that is, if a number of choices is specified by the question). You should double-check the review list for completion if you finish the section early. Using the review list feature will take some practice as well, which is why we've built it into our online practice exams. Here's some introductory advice.

The majority of test takers will be pressed for time. Thus, for most of you, it won't be feasible to "go back to" multiple problems at the end of the section. Generally, if you can't get a question the first time, you won't be able to get it the second time around either. With this in mind, here's how we recommend using the new review list feature.

1. Do the questions in order as they appear.

2. When you encounter a difficult question, do you best to eliminate answer choices you know are wrong.

3. If you're not sure of an answer, take an educated guess from the choices remaining. Do <u>NOT</u> skip it and hope to return to it later.

4. Using the "mark" button at the top of the screen, mark up to three questions per section that you think you might be able to solve with more time. Mark a question only after you have taken an educated guess.

5. If you have time at the end of the section, click on the review list, identify any questions you've marked and return to them. If you do not have any time remaining, you will have already taken good guesses at the tough ones.

What you want to avoid is "surfing"—clicking forward and backward through the questions searching for the easy ones. This will eat up valuable time. Of course, you'll want to move through the tough ones quickly if you can't get them, but try to avoid skipping stuff.

Again, all of this will take practice. Use our practice exams to fine-tune your approach.

Scoring

Two things have changed about the scoring of the Verbal Reasoning and Quantitative Reasoning sections: (1) how individual questions influence the score and (2) the score scale itself.

For both the Verbal Reasoning and Quantitative Reasoning sections, you will receive a raw score, which is simply how many questions you answered correctly. Your raw score is converted to a scaled score, accounting for the difficulties of the specific questions you actually saw.

The old GRE general section was question-adaptive, meaning that your answer to each question (right or wrong) determined, at least somewhat, the questions that followed (harder or easier). Because you had to commit to an answer to let the algorithm do its thing, you weren't allowed to skip questions or go back to change answers. On the revised GRE, the adapting will occur from section-to-section (e.g., if you do well on the first verbal section, you will get a harder second verbal section) rather than from question-to-question. The only change test takers will notice is one most will welcome: you can now move freely about the questions in a section, skipping tough questions and coming back to them later, changing answers after "ah-ha!" moments, and generally managing your time more flexibly.

The scores for the revised GRE Quantitative Reasoning and Verbal Reasoning will be reported on a 130 to 170 scale in 1-point increments, whereas the old score reporting was on a 200 to 800 scale in 10-point increments. You will receive one 130–170 score for verbal and a separate 130–170 score for quant. If you are already putting your GRE math skills to work, you may notice that there are now 41 scores possible (170 − 130, then add one before you're done), whereas before there were 61 scores possible ([800 − 200]/10, then add one before you're done). In other words, a 10 point difference on the old score scale actually indicated a smaller performance differential than a 1 point difference on the new scale. However, the GRE folks argue that perception is reality: the difference between 520 and 530 on the old scale could simply *seem* greater than the difference between 151 and 152 on the new scale. If that's true, then this change will benefit test-takers, who won't be unfairly compared by schools for minor differences in performance. If not true, then the change will be moot.

Important Dates

Registration for the GRE revised General Test opens on March 15, 2011, and the first day of testing with the new format is August 1, 2011.

Perhaps to encourage people to take the revised exam, rather than rushing to take the old exam before the change or waiting "to see what happens" with the new exam long after August 1, 2011, ETS is offering a 50% discount on the test fee for anyone who takes the revised test from August 1 through September 30, 2011. Scores for people who take the revised exam in this discount period will be sent starting in mid- to late-November. This implies that you may have to wait up to 3.5 months to get your score during this rollout period!

By December 2011, ETS expects to resume normal score reporting schedules: score reports will be sent a mere 10-15 days after the test date.

IMPORTANT: If you need GRE scores before mid-November 2011 to meet a school deadline, take the "old" GRE no later than July 31, 2011! Waiting to take the revised test not only would require you to study for a different test, but also would delay your score reporting.

Question Formats in Detail

Essay Questions

The Analytical Writing section consists of two separately timed 30-minute tasks: Analyze an Issue and Analyze an Argument. As you can imagine, the 30-minute time limit implies that you aren't aiming to write an essay that would garner a Pulitzer Prize nomination, but rather to complete the tasks adequately and according to the directions. Each essay is scored separately, but your reported essay score is the average of the two rounded *up* to the next half-point increment on a 0 to 6 scale.

Issue Task—This essay prompt will present a claim, generally one that is vague enough to be interpreted in various ways and discussed from numerous perspectives. Your job as a test taker is to write a response discussing the extent to which you agree or disagree and support your position. Don't sit on the fence—pick a side!

For some examples of Issue Task prompts, visit the GRE website here:

http://www.ets.org/gre/revised_general/prepare/analytical_writing/issue/pool

Argument Task—This essay prompt will be an argument comprised of both a claim(s) and evidence. Your job is to dispassionately discuss the argument's structural flaws and merits (well, mostly the flaws). Don't agree or disagree with the argument—evaluate its logic.

For some examples of Argument Task prompts, visit the GRE website here:

http://www.ets.org/gre/revised_general/prepare/analytical_writing/argument/pool

VERBAL: READING COMPREHENSION QUESTIONS

Standard 5-choice multiple choice reading comprehension questions will continue to appear on the new exam. You are likely familiar with how these work. Let's take a look at two *new* reading comprehension formats that will appear on the new test.

SELECT ONE OR MORE ANSWER CHOICES AND SELECT-IN-PASSAGE

For the question type, "Select One or More Answer Choices," you are given three statements about a passage and asked to "select all that apply." Either one, two, or all three can be correct (there is no "none of the above" option). There is no partial credit; you must select all the correct choices and none of the incorrect choices.

> *Strategy Tip: On "Select One or More Answer Choices," don't let your brain be tricked into telling you "Well, if two of them have been right so far, the other one must be wrong," or any other arbitrary idea about how many of the choices "should" be correct. Make sure to consider each choice independently! You cannot use "Process of Elimination" the same way as you do on "normal" multiple-choice questions.*

For the question type "Select-in-Passage," you are given an assignment such as "Select the sentence in the passage that explains why the experiment's results were discovered to be invalid." Clicking anywhere on the sentence in the passage will highlight it. (As with any GRE question, you will have to click "Confirm" to submit your answer, so don't worry about accidentally selecting the wrong sentence due to a slip of the mouse.)

> *Strategy Tip: On "Select-in-Passage," if the passage is short, consider numbering each sentence (that is, writing 1 2 3 4 on your paper) and crossing off each choice as you determine that it isn't the answer. If the passage is long, you might write a number for each paragraph (I, II, III), and tick off each number as you determine that the correct sentence is not located in that paragraph.*

Now let's give these new question types a try!

The sample questions below are based on this passage:

> Physicist Robert Oppenheimer, director of the fateful Manhattan Project, said "It is a profound and necessary truth that the deep things in science are not found because they are useful; they are found because it was possible to find them." In a later address at MIT, Oppenheimer presented the thesis that scientists could be held only very nominally responsible for the consequences of their research and discovery. Oppenheimer asserted that ethics, philosophy, and politics have very little to do with the day-to-day work of the scientist, and that scientists could not rationally be expected to predict all the effects of their work. Yet, in a talk in 1945 to the Association of Los Alamos Scientists, Oppenheimer offered some reasons why the Manhattan project scientists built the atomic bomb; the justifications included "fear that Nazi Germany would build it first" and "hope that it would shorten the war."

For question #1, consider each of the three choices separately and select all that apply.

1. The passage implies that Robert Oppenheimer would most likely have agreed with which of the following views:

> [A] Some scientists take military goals into account in their work
> [B] Deep things in science are not useful
> [C] The everyday work of a scientist is only minimally involved with ethics

2. Select the sentence in which the writer implies that Oppenheimer has not been consistent in his view that scientists have little consideration for the effects of their work.

[Here, you would highlight the appropriate sentence with your mouse. Note that there are only four options.]

Solutions:

1. {A, C} Oppenheimer says in the last sentence that one of the reasons the bomb was built was scientists' "hope that it would shorten the war." Thus, Oppenheimer would likely agree with the view that "Some scientists take military goals into account in their work." B is a trap answer using familiar language from the passage. Oppenheimer says that scientific discoveries' possible usefulness is not why scientists make discoveries; he does not say that the discoveries aren't useful. Oppenheimer specifically says that ethics has "very little to do with the day-to-day work of the scientist," which is a good match for "only minimally involved with ethics."

    Strategy Tip: On "Select One or More Answer Choices," write ABC on your paper and mark each choice with a check, an X, or a symbol such as ~ if you're not sure. This should keep you from crossing out all three choices and having to go back (at least one of the choices must be correct). For example, let's say that on a different question you had marked

        A. X
        B. X
        C. ~

    The one you weren't sure about, (C), is likely to be correct, since there must be at least one correct answer.

2. The correct sentence is: **Yet, in a talk in 1945 to the Association of Los Alamos Scientists, Oppenheimer offered some reasons why the Manhattan project scientists built the atomic bomb; the justifications included "fear that Nazi Germany would build it first" and "hope that it would shorten the war."** The word "yet" is a good clue that this sentence is about to express a view contrary to the views expressed in the rest of the passage.

Verbal: Text Completion Questions

Text Completions are the new, souped-up Sentence Completions. They can consist of 1–5 sentences with 1–3 blanks. When Text Completions have two or three blanks, you will select words for those blanks independently. There is no partial credit; you must make every selection correctly.

Because this makes things a bit harder, the GRE has kindly reduced the number of possible choices per blank from five to three. Here is an old two-blank Sentence Completion, as it would appear on the old GRE:

Old Format:

Leaders are not always expected to _____ the same rules as are those they lead; leaders are often looked up to for a surety and presumption that would be viewed as _____ in most others.

        A. obey ... avarice

        B. proscribe ... insalubriousness

        C. decree ... anachronism

        D. conform to ... hubris

        E. follow ... eminence

And here's how this same sentence would appear on the new exam.

New Format:

Leaders are not always expected to (i) _____ the same rules as are those they lead; leaders are often looked up to for a surety and presumption that would be viewed as (ii) _____ in most others.

Blank (i)
decree
proscribe
conform to

Blank (ii)
hubris
avarice
anachronism

On the new GRE, you will select your two choices by actually clicking and highlighting the words you want.

Solution:

In the first blank, we need a word similar to "follow." In the second blank, we need a word similar to "arrogant." Only choice D works in the old format; in the new format, the answer is still "conform to" and "hubris," but you'll make the two choices separately.

Note that in the "Old Format" question, if you knew that you needed a word in the second blank that meant something like "arrogant," and you knew that "hubris" was the only word in the second column with the correct meaning, you could pick correct answer choice D without even considering the first word in each pair. In the new format, this strategy is no longer available to us.

Also note that, in the "Old Format" question, "obey," "conform to," and "follow" mean basically the same thing. On the new GRE, this can't happen: since you select each word independently, no two choices can be synonyms (otherwise, there would be two correct answers).

Strategy Tip: As on the old GRE, do NOT look at the answer choices until you've decided for yourself, based on textual clues actually written in the sentence, what kind of word needs to go in each blank. Only then should you look at the choices and eliminate those that are not matches.

Let's try an example with three blanks.

For Kant, the fact of having a right and having the (i) _____ to enforce it via coercion cannot be separated, and he asserts that this marriage of rights and coercion is compatible with the freedom of everyone. This is not at all peculiar from the standpoint of modern political thought—what good is a right if its violation triggers no enforcement (be it punishment or (ii) _____)? The necessity of coercion is not at all in conflict with the freedom of everyone, because this coercion only comes into play when someone has (iii)_____ someone else.

Blank (ii)
technique
license
prohibition

Blank (ii)
amortization
reward
restitution

Blank (iii)
questioned the hypothesis of
violated the rights of
granted civil liberties to

Solution:

In the first sentence, use the clue "he asserts that this marriage of rights and coercion is compatible with the freedom of everyone" to help fill in the first blank. Kant believes that "coercion" is "married to" rights and is compatible with freedom for all. So we want something in the first blank like "right" or "power." Kant believes that rights are meaningless without enforcement. Only the choice "license" can work (while a "license" can be physical, like a driver's license, "license" can also mean "right").

The second blank is part of the phrase "punishment or _____," which we are told is the "enforcement" resulting from the violation of a right. So the blank should be something, other than punishment, that constitutes enforcement against someone who violates a right. (More simply, it should be something bad!) Only "restitution" works. Restitution is compensating the victim in some way (perhaps monetarily or by returning stolen goods).

In the final sentence, "coercion only comes into play when someone has _____ someone else." Throughout the text, "coercion" means enforcement against someone who has violated the rights of someone else. The meaning is the same here. The answer is "violated the rights of."

The complete and correct answer is this combination:

| Blank (i) | Blank (ii) | Blank (iii) |
| license | restitution | violated the rights of |

In theory, there are $3 \times 3 \times 3 = 27$ possible ways to answer a 3-blank Text Completion—and only one of those 27 ways is correct. The guessing odds will go down, but don't be intimidated. Just follow the basic process: come up with your own filler for each blank, and match to the answer choices. If you're confused by this example, don't worry! We'll start from the beginning in our *Text Completion & Sentence Equivalence* strategy guide.

Strategy Tip: As on the old GRE, do NOT "write your own story." The GRE cannot give you a blank without also giving you a clue, physically written down in the passage, telling you what kind of word or phrase MUST go in that blank. Find that clue. You should be able to give textual evidence for each answer choice you select.

Verbal: Sentence Equivalence Questions

In this question type, you are given one sentence with a single blank. There are six answer choices, and you are asked to pick TWO choices that fit the blank and are alike in meaning.

Of the new question types, this one depends the most on vocabulary and also yields the most to strategy.

No partial credit is given on Sentence Equivalence; both correct answers must be selected. When you pick two of six choices, there are 15 possible combinations of choices, and only one is correct. However, this is not nearly as daunting as it sounds.

Think of it this way—if you have six choices, but the two correct ones must be "similar in meaning," then you have, at most, three possible PAIRS of choices. Maybe fewer, since not all choices are guaranteed to have a "partner." If you can match up the "pairs," you can seriously narrow down your options.

Here is a sample set of answer choices:

- [A] tractable
- [B] taciturn
- [C] arbitrary
- [D] tantamount
- [E] reticent
- [F] amenable

We haven't even given you the question here, because we want to point out how much you can do with the choices alone, if you have studied vocabulary sufficiently.

TRACTABLE and AMENABLE are synonyms (tractable, amenable people will do whatever you want them to do). TACITURN and RETICENT are synonyms (both mean "not talkative"). ARBITRARY (based on one's own will) and TANTAMOUT (equivalent) are not similar in meaning and therefore cannot be a pair. Therefore, the ONLY possible answers are {A, F} and {B, E}. We have improved our chances from 1 in 15 to a 50/50 shot without even reading the question!

Of course, in approaching a Sentence Equivalence, we do want to analyze the sentence the same way we would with a Text Completion—read for a textual clue that tells you what type of word MUST go in the blank. Then look for a matching pair.

Strategy Tip: If you're sure that a word in the choices does NOT have a partner, cross it out! For instance, if A and C are partners, and E and F are partners, and you're sure B and D are not each other's partners, cross out B and D completely. They cannot be the answer together, nor can either one be part of the answer.

The sentence for the answer choice above could read,

> Though the dinner guests were quite _____ , the hostess did her best to keep the conversation active and engaging.

Thus, B and E are the best choices. Let's try an example.

While athletes usually expect to achieve their greatest feats in their teens or twenties, opera singers don't reach the _____ of their vocal powers until middle age.

- [A] harmony
- [B] zenith
- [C] acme
- [D] terminus
- [E] nadir
- [F] cessation

Solution:

Those with strong vocabularies might go straight to the choices to make pairs. ZENITH and ACME are synonyms, meaning "high point, peak." TERMINUS and CESSATION are synonyms, meaning "end." NADIR is a low point and HARMONY is present here as a trap answer reminding us of opera singers. *Cross off A and E, since they do not have partners.* Then, go back to the sentence, knowing that your only options are a pair meaning "peak" and a pair meaning "end."

The answer is {B, C}.

Math: Quantitative Comparison

This format is a holdover from the old exam. Here's a quick example:

Quantity A	Quantity B
x	x^2

   (A) Quantity A is greater.
   (B) Quantity B is greater.
   (C) The two quantities are equal.
   (D) The relationship cannot be determined from the information given.

Solution: If $x = 0$, the quantities are equal. If $x = 2$, quantity B is greater. Thus, we don't have enough information.

The answer is D.

Let's look at the new math question formats.

Math: Select One or More Answer Choices

According to the *Official Guide to the GRE Revised General Test*, the official directions for "Select One or More Answer Choices" read as follows:

> Directions: Select one or more answer choices according to the specific question directions.
>
> If the question does not specify how many answer choices to select, select all that apply.
>
> The correct answer may be just one of the choices or as many as all of the choices, depending on the question.
>
> No credit is given unless you select all of the correct choices and no others.
>
> If the question specifies how many answer choices to select, select exactly that number of choices.

Note that there is no "partial credit." If three of six choices are correct and you select two of the three, no credit is given. It will also be important to read the directions carefully.

That said, many of these questions look *very* similar to those on the "old" GRE. For instance, here is a question that could have appeared on the GRE in the past:

> If $ab = |a| \times |b|$, which of the following *must* be true?
>
> I. $a = b$
> II. $a > 0$ and $b > 0$
> III. $ab > 0$
>
> A.   II only
> B.   III only
> C.   I and III only
> D.   II and III only
> E.   I, II, and III

Solution: If $ab = |a| \times |b|$, then we know ab is positive, since the right side of the equation must be positive. If ab is positive, however, that doesn't necessarily mean that a and b are each positive; it simply means that they have the same sign.

> I.   It is not true that a must equal b. For instance, a could be 2 and b could be 3.
> II.   It is not true that a and b must each be positive. For instance, a could be -3 and b could be -4.
> III.   True. Since $|a| \times |b|$ must be positive, ab must be positive as well.

The answer is B (III only).

Note that, if you determined that statement I was false, you could eliminate choices C and E before considering the remaining statements. Then, if you were confident that II was also false, you could safely pick answer choice B, III only, without even trying statement III, since "None of the above" isn't an option. That is, because of the multiple choice answers, it is sometimes not necessary to consider each statement individually. This is the aspect of such problems that will change on the new exam.

Here is the same problem, in the new format.

> If $ab = |a| \times |b|$, which of the following *must* be true?
>
> Indicate <u>all</u> such statements.
>
> [A] $a = b$
> [B] $a > 0$ and $b > 0$
> [C] $ab > 0$

Strategy Tip: Make sure to fully "process" the statement in the question (simplify it or list the possible scenarios) before considering the answer choices. This will save you time in the long run!

Here, we would simply select choice C. The only thing that has changed is that we can't do process of elimination; we must always consider each statement individually. On the upside, the problem has become much more straightforward and compact (not every real-life problem has exactly five possible solutions; why should those on the GRE?).

MATH: NUMERIC ENTRY

This question type requires the text taker to key a numeric answer into a box on the screen. You are not able to "work backwards" from answer choices, and in many cases it will be difficult to make a guess. However, the principles being tested are the same as on the old GRE.

Here is a sample question:

If $x*y = 2xy - (x - y)$, what is the value of $3*4$?

Solution:

We are given a function involving two variables, x and y, and asked to substitute 3 for x and 4 for y:

$$x*y = 2xy - (x - y)$$
$$3*4 = 2(3)(4) - (3 - 4)$$
$$3*4 = 24 - (-1)$$
$$3*4 = 25$$

The answer is 25.

Thus, you would type 25 into the box.

Okay. You've now got a good start on understanding the structure and question formats of the new GRE. Now it's time to begin fine-tuning your skills.

Chapter 2
of
WORD PROBLEMS

ALGEBRAIC TRANSLATIONS

In This Chapter . . .

ALGEBRAIC TRANSLATIONS

In This Chapter:

- Understanding what word problems are asking
- *Translating* word problems into *algebra* (equations, inequalities, expressions, etc.)

Decoding the GRE Word Problem

Two thoughts are common to many frustrated students:

"I don't know where to get started" and "I don't know what they want me to do."

Let's attack these frustrations one at a time.

"I don't know where to get started."

A *passive thinker* takes in information, hopes that it will lead somewhere, waits for a connection to appear and then… (hopefully)… *voila!* In contrast, the *active thinker aggressively* seeks out relationships between the various elements of a problem and looks to write equations which can be solved. *You have to be an active thinker on the GRE.*

Let's look at a sample problem:

> A steel rod 50 meters long is cut into two pieces. If one piece is 14 meters longer than the other, what is the length, in meters, of the shorter piece?

The trick to word problems is to not try to do everything all at once. While it's great when the entire process is clear from the start, such clarity about your work is often not the case. That's why **we need to start by identifying unknowns and creating variables to represent the unknowns.** What quantities have we not been given specific values for? Take a moment to identify those quantities and write them down in the space provided below. Make up letters (variables) to stand for the quantities, and label these letters.

Identify Unknowns and Create Variables

In this question, both the <u>length of the shorter piece</u> and the <u>length of the longer piece</u> are unknown, so let's begin by assigning each of those values a variable. We could go with the traditional algebraic variables x and y, but what if we forget which is which while we're busy answering the question? Instead, let's use letters that can help us remember which variable is assigned to which value:

S = length of the shorter piece
L = length of the longer piece

Just like that, we've gotten started on this problem. This may seem like a minor accomplishment in terms of the entire question, but it was an important one. Often, as soon as you start translating a word problem <u>into algebra</u>, the path forward becomes clearer. Now it's time to deal with our second frustration.

"I don't know what they want me to do."

Even now that we've identified and labeled our variables, you might still feel confused. That's fine. Virtually everyone ends up facing a number of problems that are above his or her ability level on the GRE. What distinguishes the higher-performing GRE test-takers in these moments is that they begin spelling out relationships before they know how the equations will prove useful. It's similar to untangling a ball of yarn: if you waited until you knew how the entire process would end, you might never get started. Of course, you hope to have a clear vision right from the start, but if you don't, *dive in and see what you find*—you'll likely make key realizations along the way. Ironically, often it's the road blocks we encounter that point the way. So our next step is to **identify relationships and create equations.**

Let's go back to our problem, look at *one piece of information at a time*, and *start translating that information into equations.* Try it first on your own, then we'll go through it together.

A steel rod 50 meters long is cut into two pieces.

The relationship expressed here is one of the two most common types of relationships found in word problems. We know the original length of the rod was 50 meters, and we know that it was cut into 2 pieces. Therefore, we know that the length of the shorter piece plus the length of the longer piece must equal 50 meters. This common relationship (one you should watch out for in other word problems) is **Parts Add to a Sum**. So a good way to express this relationship algebraically would be to write:

$S + L = 50$

Now that we've translated the first part of the problem, let's move on to the next part.

If one piece is 14 meters longer than the other...

The relationship expressed here is another common type found in word problems. The longer piece of metal is 14 meters longer than the shorter piece of metal. So if we were to add 14 meters to the shorter piece, it would be the same length as the longer piece. This relationship (be on the lookout for this one too) is **One Part Can Be Made Equal to the Other**. Either the question will say that two values are equivalent, or it will tell you exactly *how they differ.* This question told us how they were different, so our equation shows how we could make them equivalent. In this case, we would want to say:

$S + 14 = L$

By the way, when constructing equations in which you are making one part equal to the other, it can be very easy to express the relationship backwards. If you mistakenly wrote down $S = L + 14$, you're not alone. A good habit to get into if you find yourself making this kind of error is to verify your equation with **hypothetical numbers.** To check if my equation above is correct, I'm going to start by imagining that my shorter piece of metal is 20 meters long. If the shorter piece were 20 meters long, then the longer piece would have to be 34 meters long. Now I plug those numbers into my equation. Does $(20) + 14 = (34)$? Yes, it does, so my equation is correct.x

Let's move on to the final part of the question.

> *…what is the length, in meters, of the shorter piece?*

This part of the question doesn't describe a relationship that we can use to create an equation, but it does tell us something quite useful: it tells us *what we're solving for!* Make sure that you note in some way what value you're actually looking for as you solve a problem—it can help you stay focused on the task at hand. In this problem, we're trying to find *S*.

On your paper, you might even write:

$$S = ?$$

So now that we've **identified** our **unknowns and created variables**, **identified relationships** and **created equations,** and **identified what the question is asking for,** it's time to put the pieces together and answer the question. Try it on your own first, and then when you've got an answer, turn the page and we'll go through the final steps together.

Let's recap, and then we'll complete the final steps and answer the question. After reading the question, we were able to create 2 equations:

$$S + L = 50$$
$$S + 14 = L$$

We've been in this situation before. We have 2 variables and 2 equations. It's time to solve for S.

$$S + L = 50 \;\rightarrow\; L = 50 - S$$

$$S + 14 = (50 - S)$$

$$S + 14 = 50 - S$$
$$\underline{-14 \quad -14}$$

$$S = 36 - S$$
$$\underline{+S \qquad +S}$$

$$\frac{2S}{2} = \frac{36}{2}$$
$$S = 18$$

If you had trouble getting the correct value for S, then you should probably go back and refresh your algebra skills (see our Algebra guide). Knowing how to substitute and solve is absolutely essential if you want to do consistently well on word problems. If you're comfortable with everything we've done so far in order to answer the question, then you're ready for a tougher problem.

> Jack is 13 years older than Ben. In 8 years, he will be twice as old as Ben. How old is Jack now?

First try this problem on your own. Remember to follow the same steps we followed in the last question. After you're finished, we'll go through it together on the next page.

Ok, let's get started. The first thing we have to do is **identify** our **unknowns** and **create variables**. In this problem, the two unknowns are the ages of Jack and Ben. We can represent them like this:

J = Jack's age NOW
B = Ben's age NOW

Before we move on to the next step, it's important to understand why we want to specify that our variables represent Jack and Ben's ages NOW. As you were solving this problem by yourself, you may have noticed that there was an added wrinkle to this question. We are presented with information that describes 2 distinct points in time—now and 8 years from now. Some word problems on the GRE provide information about 2 distinct but related situations. When you are dealing with one of those problems, be careful about the reference point for your variables. In this case, we want to say that our variables represent Jack and Ben's ages *now* as opposed to 8 years from now. This makes it easier to express their ages at other points in time.

Now that we've created our variables, it's time to **identify relationships** and **create equations**. Let's go through the information presented in the question one piece at a time.

Jack is 13 years older than Ben.

Once again, we should check that we're putting this together the right way (not putting the +13 on the wrong side of the equation). Our equation should be

$J = B + 13$, **NOT** $J + 13 = B$

Let's move on to the next piece of information.

In 8 years, he will be twice as old as Ben.

This piece is more challenging to translate than you might otherwise suspect. Remember, our variables represent their ages now, but this statement is talking about their ages 8 years from now. So we can't just write $J = 2B$. This relationship is dependent upon Jack and Ben's ages 8 years from now. We don't want to use new variables to represent these different ages, so let's adjust the values like this:

$(J + 8)$ = Jack's age 8 years from now
$(B + 8)$ = Ben's age 8 years from now

Now we can accurately create equations related to the earlier time *and* to the later time. Plus, if we keep those values in parentheses, then we can avoid potential PEMDAS errors! So our second equation should read:

$(J + 8) = 2(B + 8)$

Only one more piece of the question to go:

How old is Jack now?

This tells us that we're looking for the value of J. In other words, $J =$?. All the pieces are in place and we're ready to solve.

$(J + 8) = 2(B + 8) \rightarrow J + 8 = 2B + 16$	Simplify grouped terms
$J = B + 13 \rightarrow J - 13 = B$	Isolate the variable you want to eliminate

$$J + 8 = 2(J - 13) + 16$$ Substitute into the other equation

$$J + 8 = 2J - 26 + 16$$ Simplify grouped terms

$$
\begin{array}{r}
J + 8 = 2J - 10 \\
-J + 10 \quad -J + 10 \\
\hline
18 = \quad J
\end{array}
$$

The question asks for Jack's age, so we have our answer. Let's review what we know about word problems and the steps we should take to solve them.

Step 1: Identify unknowns and create variables.

- Don't forget to use descriptive letters (e.g., shorter piece = S).

- Be <u>very specific</u> when dealing with questions that contain 2 distinct but related situations (i.e. Jack's age NOW = J vs. Jack's age in 8 years = $J + 8$).

Step 2: Identify relationships and create equations.

- As a general guideline, once you have identified how many unknowns (variables) you have, that will give you a big clue as to how many equations you will ultimately need. If you have 2 variables, you will need 2 equations to be able to find unique values for those variables.

- Don't forget to look at one piece of the question at a time. Don't try to do everything at once!

- Use numbers to check that you have set up your equation correctly. For example, if they say that Jack is twice as old as Ben, which is correct: $J = 2B$ or $2J = B$? If Jack were 40, Ben would be 20, so $(40) = 2(20)$ or $2(40) = 20$?

Step 3: Identify what the question is asking for.

- Having a clear goal can prevent you from losing track of what you're doing and can help you stay focused on the task at hand.

Step 4: Solve for the <u>wanted</u> element (often by using substitution).

- The ability to perform every step accurately and efficiently is critical to success on the GRE. Make sure to answer the **right question**—practice makes perfect!

Now that we've gone through the basic steps, it's time to practice translating word problems into equations. But first, here are some common mathematical relationships found on the GRE, words and phrases you might find used to describe them, and their translations. Use them to help you with the drill sets at the end of this chapter.

Common Word Problem Phrases

Addition
Add, Sum, Total (of parts), More Than: +
The sum of x and y: $x + y$
The sum of the three funds combined: $a + b + c$
When fifty is added to his age: $a + 50$
Six pounds heavier than Dave: $d + 6$
A group of men and women: $m + w$
The cost is marked up: $c + m$

Subtraction
Minus, Difference, Less Than: −
x minus five: $x - 5$
The difference between Quentin's and Rachel's heights (if Quentin is taller): $q - r$
Four pounds less than expected: $e - 4$
The profit is the revenue minus the cost: $P = R - C$

Multiplication
The product of h and k: $h \times k$
The number of reds times the number of blues: $r \times b$
One fifth of y: $(1/5) \times y$
n persons have x beads each: total number of beads $= nx$
Go z miles per hour for t hours: distance $= zt$ miles

Ratios and Division
Quotient, Per, Ratio, Proportion: ÷ or /
Five dollars every two weeks: (5 dollars/2 weeks) → 2.5 dollars a week
The ratio of x to y: x/y
The proportion of girls to boys: g/b

Average or Mean (sum of terms divided by the total number of terms)
The average of a and b: $\dfrac{a+b}{2}$

The average salary of the three doctors: $\dfrac{x+y+z}{3}$

A student's average score on 5 tests was 87: $\dfrac{\text{sum}}{5} = 87$ or $\dfrac{a+b+c+d+e}{5} = 87$

Translating Words Correctly

1. Avoid writing relationships backwards.

If You See...		Write:		Not:
"A is half the size of B"	✓	$A = \frac{1}{2}B$	✗	$B = \frac{1}{2}A$
"A is 5 less than B"	✓	$A = B - 5$	✗	$A = 5 - B$
"A is less than B"	✓	$A < B$	✗	$A > B$
"Jane bought twice as many apples as bananas"	✓	$A = 2B$	✗	$2A = B$

2. Quickly check your translation with easy numbers.

For the last example above, you might think the following:

> "Jane bought twice as many apples as bananas. More apples than bananas. Say she buys 5 bananas. She buys twice as many apples—that's 10 apples. Makes sense. So the equation is Apples equals 2 times Bananas, or $A = 2B$, not the other way around."

These numbers do not have to satisfy any other conditions of the problem. Use these "quick picks" only to test the form of your translation.

3. Write an unknown percent as a variable divided by 100.

If You See...	Write	Not
"P is X percent of Q"	✓ $P = \frac{X}{100}Q$ or $\frac{P}{Q} = \frac{X}{100}$	✗ $P = X\%Q$ (cannot be manipulated)

4. Translate bulk discounts and similar relationships carefully.

If You See...	Write	Not
"Pay \$10 per CD for the first 2 CDs, then \$7 per additional CD"	✓ n = # of CDs bought T = total amount paid (\$) $T = \$10 \times 2 + \$7 \times (n - 2)$ (assuming $n > 2$)	✗ $T = \$10 \times 2 + \$7 \times n$

Always pay attention to the *meaning* of the sentence you are translating! If necessary, *take a few extra seconds* to make *sure* you've set up the algebra correctly.

Check Your Skills

Translate the following statements:

1. Lily is two years older than Melissa.
2. A small pizza costs $5 less than a large pizza.
3. Twice *A* is 5 more than *B*.
4. *R* is 45 percent of *Q*.
5. John has more than twice as many CDs as Ken.

Answers may be found on page 37.

Hidden Constraints

Notice that in some problems, there is a **hidden constraint** on the possible quantities. This would apply, for instance, to the number of apples and bananas that Jane bought. Since each fruit is a physical, countable object, you can only have a **whole number** of each type. Whole numbers are the integers 0, 1, 2, and so on. So you can have 1 apples, 2 apples, 3 apples, etc., and even 0 apples, but you cannot have fractional apples or negative apples.

As a result of this implied "whole number" constraint, you often have more information than you might think and you may be able to answer a question with fewer facts.

Consider the following example:

> If Kelly received 1/3 more votes than Mike in a student election, which of the following could have been the total number of votes cast for the two candidates?
>
> (A) 12   (B) 13   (C) 14   (D) 15   (E) 16

Let M be the number of votes cast for Mike. Then Kelly received $M + (1/3)M$, or $(4/3)M$ votes. The total number of votes cast was therefore "votes for Mike" plus "votes for Kelly," or $M + (4/3)M$. This quantity equals $(7/3)M$, or $7M/3$.

Because M is a number of votes, it cannot be a fraction—specifically, not a fraction with a 7 in the denominator. Therefore, the 7 in the expression $7M/3$ cannot be cancelled out. As a result, the total number of votes cast must be a multiple of 7. Among the answer choices, the only multiple of 7 is 14, so the correct answer is (**C**).

Another way to solve this problem is this: the number of votes cast for Mike (M) must be a multiple of 3, since the total number of votes is a whole number. So $M = 3, 6, 9$, etc. Kelly received 1/3 more votes, so the number of votes she received is 4, 8, 12, etc. Thus the total number of votes is 7, 14, 21, etc.

Not every unknown quantity related to real objects is restricted to whole numbers. Many physical measurements, such as weights, times, or speeds, can be any positive number, not necessarily integers. A few quantities can even be negative (e.g., temperatures, *x*- or *y*-coordinates). Think about what is being measured or counted, and you will recognize whether a hidden constraint applies.

Check Your Skills

Translate the following statements:

6. In a certain word, the number of consonants is 1/4 more than the number of vowels. Which of the following is a possibility for the number of letters in the word?
   (A) 8   (B) 9   (C) 10   (D) 11   (E) 12

Answers may be found on page 37.

Check Your Skills Answers

1. $L = M + 2$

2. $S = L - 5$

3. $2A = B + 5$

4. $R = \dfrac{45}{100} \times Q$ or $R = 0.45\,Q$

5. $J > 2K$

6. **B:** There is a hidden constraint in this question. The number of vowels and the number of consonants must both be integers. The number of consonants is 1/4 more than the number of vowels, which means we need to multiply the number of vowels by 1/4 to determine how many more consonants there are. If we label the number of vowels v, then there are $v/4$ more consonants than vowels. The only way that $v/4$ will be an integer is if v is a multiple of 4.

If $v = 4$, there is $(4)/4 = 1$ more consonant than there are vowels, so there are $4 + 1 = 5$ consonants. That gives a total of $4 + 5 = 9$ letters in the word. The correct answer is B.

Problem Set

Solve the following problems with the four-step method outlined in this section.

1. John is 20 years older than Brian. 12 years ago, John was twice as old as Brian. How old is Brian?

2. Mrs. Miller has two dogs, Jackie and Stella, who weigh a total of 75 pounds. If Stella weighs 15 pounds less than twice Jackie's weight, how much does Stella weigh?

3. Caleb spends $72.50 on 50 hamburgers for the marching band. If single burgers cost $1.00 each and double burgers cost $1.50 each, how many double burgers did he buy?

4. United Telephone charges a base rate of $10.00 for service, plus an additional charge of $0.25 per minute. Atlantic Call charges a base rate of $12.00 for service, plus an additional charge of $0.20 per minute. For what number of minutes would the bills for each telephone company be the same?

5. Carla cuts a 70-inch piece of ribbon into 2 pieces. If the first piece is five inches more than one fourth as long as the second piece, how long is the longer piece of ribbon?

6. Jane started baby-sitting when she was 18 years old. Whenever she baby-sat for a child, that child was no more than half her age at the time. Jane is currently 32 years old, and she stopped baby-sitting 10 years ago. What is the current age of the oldest person for whom Jane could have baby-sat?

7.

Ten years ago, Brian was twice
as old as Aubrey.

Quantity A	**Quantity B**
Twice Aubrey's age today	Brian's age today

8.

The length of a rectangular
room is 8 feet greater than its
width. The total area of the
room is 240 square feet.

Quantity A	**Quantity B**
The width of the room in feet	12

9.

John earns a yearly base salary of $30,000, plus a commission of $500 on every car he sells above his monthly minimum of two cars. Last year, John met or surpassed his minimum sales every month, and earned a total income (salary plus commission) of $60,000.

Quantity A

The number of cars John sold last year

Quantity B

90

1. **32:** Use an age chart to assign variables. Represent Brian's age now with b. Then John's age now is $b + 20$.

	12 years ago	Now
John	$b + 8$	$b + 20$
Brian	$b - 12$	$b = ?$

Subtract 12 from the "now" column to get the "12 years ago" column.

Then write an equation to represent the remaining information: 12 years ago, John was twice as old as Brian. Solve for b:

$$b + 8 = 2(b - 12)$$
$$b + 8 = 2b - 24$$
$$32 = b$$

You could also solve this problem by inspection. John is 20 years older than Brian. We also need John to be *twice* Brian's age at a particular point in time. Since John is always 20 years older, then he must be 40 years old at that time (and Brian must be 20 years old). This point in time was 12 years ago, so Brian is now 32 years old.

2. **45 pounds:**

Let j = Jackie's weight, and let s = Stella's weight. Stella's weight is the Ultimate Unknown: $s = ?$

(1) The two dogs weigh a total of 75 pounds:
$$j + s = 75$$

(2) Stella weighs 15 pounds less than twice Jackie's weight:
$$s = 2j - 15$$

Combine the two equations by substituting the value for s from equation (2) into equation (1):

$$j + (2j - 15) = 75$$
$$3j - 15 = 75$$
$$3j = 90$$
$$j = 30$$

Find Stella's weight by substituting Jackie's weight into equation (1):

$$30 + s = 75$$
$$s = 45$$

3. **45 double burgers:**

Let s = the number of single burgers purchased
Let d = the number of double burgers purchased

Caleb bought 50 burgers:
$$s + d = 50$$

Caleb spent \$72.50 in all:
$$s + 1.5d = 72.50$$

Combine the two equations by subtracting equation (1) from equation (2).

$$\begin{array}{r} s + 1.5d = 72.50 \\ - (s + d = 50) \\ \hline 0.5d = 22.5 \\ d = 45 \end{array}$$

4. 40 minutes:

Let x = the number of minutes.

A call made by United Telephone costs $10.00 plus $0.25 per minute: $10 + 0.25x$.

A call made by Atlantic Call costs $12.00 plus $0.20 per minute: $12 + 0.20x$.

Set the expressions equal to each other:

$$10 + 0.25x = 12 + 0.20x$$
$$0.05x = 2$$
$$x = \frac{2}{0.05} = \frac{200}{5} = 40$$

5. 52 inches:

Let x = the 1st piece of ribbon
Let y = the 2nd piece of ribbon

The ribbon is 70 inches long.

$$x + y = 70$$

The 1st piece is 5 inches more than 1/4 as long as the 2nd.

$$x = 5 + \frac{y}{4}$$

Combine the equations by substituting the value of x from equation (2) into equation (1):

$$5 + \frac{y}{4} + y = 70$$

$$20 + y + 4y = 280$$

$$5y = 260$$

$$y = 52 \quad \text{Now, since } x + y = 70, x = 18. \text{ This tells us that } x < y, \text{ so } y \text{ is the answer.}$$

6. 23: Since you are given actual ages for Jane, the easiest way to solve the problem is to think about the extreme scenarios. At one extreme, 18-year-old Jane could have baby-sat a child of age 9. Since Jane is now 32, that child would now be 23. At the other extreme, 22-year-old Jane could have baby-sat a child of age 11. Since Jane is now 32 that child would now be 21. We can see that the first scenario yields the oldest possible current age (23) of a child that Jane baby-sat.

7. A: Let A and B denote Aubrey and Brian's ages today. Then, their ages 10 years ago would be given by $A - 10$ and $B - 10$, respectively. Those ages are related by the problem statement as:

$$B - 10 = 2(A - 10)$$

Expanding and simplifying yields

$$B - 10 = 2A - 20$$
$$B = 2A - 10$$

Rewrite the quantities in terms of A and B. Twice Aubrey's age today is $2A$ and Brian's age today is B.

Quantity A	**Quantity B**
Twice Aubrey's age today = **2A**	Brian's age today = **B**

According to the equation, B is 10 less than $2A$. Therefore the value in **Quantity A is larger.**

8. **C:** Let L and W stand for the length and width of the room in feet. Then, from the first relation, we can write this equation:

$$L = W + 8$$

Moreover, the area of a rectangle is given by length times width, such that:

$$LW = 240$$

Taken together, we have two equations with two unknowns, and because the question involves the width rather than the length, we should eliminate the length by substituting from the first equation into the second:

$$(W + 8)W = 240$$

We can now expand the product and move everything to the left hand side, so that we may solve the quadratic equation by factoring it. This gives:

$$W^2 + 8W = 240$$
$$W^2 + 8W - 240 = 0$$
$$(W + 20)(W - 12) = 0$$

The two solutions are $W = -20$ and $W = 12$. A negative width does not make sense, so W must equal 12 feet.

It is also possible to arrive at the answer by testing the value in Quantity B as the width of the room. Plug in 12 for W in the first equation

$$L = (12) + 8 = 20 \text{ feet}$$

If $W = 12$ and $L = 20$, then the area is $(20)(12) = 240$ square feet. Because this agrees with the given fact, we may conclude that 12 feet is indeed the width of the room.

Either method arrives at the conclusion that the **two quantities are equal.**

9. **B:** The simplest method for solving a problem like this is to work backwards from the value in Quantity B. Suppose John sold exactly 90 cars. Then, since he met or surpassed his minimum sales each month (which add up to 24 cars in the entire year), he would have sold another $90 - 24 = 66$ cars above the minimum.

The commission he earned on those cars is calculated as follows:

$500 \times 66 = \$33,000$

This would put his total yearly income at $30,000 (base salary) + $33,000 (commission) = $63,000. However, we know that John actually earned less than that; therefore, he must have sold fewer than 90 cars.

Quantity A	**Quantity B**
The number of cars John sold last year = **less than 90**	90

Therefore **Quantity B is greater.**

The alternative approach is to translate John's total earnings into an algebraic expression. Suppose John sold N cars. Once again, noting that he met or surpassed his monthly minimum sales, we would need to subtract 24 cars that do not contribute to his bonus from this total, and then solve for N as follows:

$$\$60,000 = \$30,000 + \$500 \times (N - 24)$$
$$\$30,000 = \$500 \times (N - 24)$$
$$60 = N - 24$$
$$84 = N$$

g

Chapter 3

of

Word Problems

RATES & WORK

In This Chapter . . .

- Basic Motion: The RTD Chart
- Matching Units in the RTD Chart
- Multiple Rates Problems
- Average Rate: Don't Just Add and Divide
- Work Problems
- Population Problems

RATES & WORK

The GRE's favorite Word Translation type is the RATE problem. Rate problems come in a variety of forms on the GRE, but all are marked by three primary components: RATE, TIME, & DISTANCE or WORK.

These three elements are related by the equation:

$$\textbf{Rate} \times \textbf{Time} = \textbf{Distance}$$
$$\text{or} \qquad \textbf{Rate} \times \textbf{Time} = \textbf{Work}$$

These equations can be abbreviated as $RT = D$ or as $RT = W$. Basic rate problems involve simple manipulations of these equations.

Note that rate-of-travel problems (with a physical distance) and work problems are really the same from the point of view of the math. The main difference is that for work problems, the right side of the equation is not a distance but an *output* (e.g., hamburgers cooked). Also, the rate is measured not in units of distance per unit of time (e.g., 10 miles per hour), but in units of *output* per unit of time (e.g., 5 hamburgers cooked per minute).

Rate problems on the GRE come in four main forms:

(1)   Motion Problems
(2)   Average Rate Problems
(3)   Work Problems
(4)   Population Problems

Basic Motion: The RTD Chart

All basic motion problems involve three elements: Rate, Time, and Distance.

Rate is expressed as a ratio of distance and time, with two corresponding units.
Some examples of rates include: 30 miles per hour, 10 meters/second, 15 kilometers/day, etc.

Time is expressed using a unit of time.
Some examples of times include: 6 hours, 23 seconds, 5 months, etc.

Distance is expressed using a unit of distance.
Some examples of distances include: 18 miles, 20 meters, 100 kilometers, etc.

You can make an "RTD chart" to solve a basic motion problem. Read the problem and fill in two of the variables. Then use the $RT = D$ formula to find the missing variable.

> If a car is traveling at 30 miles per hour, how long does it take to travel 75 miles?

An RTD chart is shown to the right. Fill in your RTD chart with the given information. Then solve for the time:

$30t = 75$, or $t = 2.5$ hours

	Rate (mi/hr)	×	Time (hr)	=	Distance (mi)
Car	30 mi/hr	×	t (hr)	=	75 mi

Matching Units in the RTD Chart

All the units in your RTD chart must match up with one another. The two units in the rate should match up with the unit of time and the unit of distance.

For example:

> It takes an elevator four seconds to go up one floor. How many floors will the elevator rise in two minutes?

	R (floors/sec)	×	T (min)	=	W (floors)
Elevator	0.25	×	2	=	?

The rate is 1 floor/4 seconds, which simplifies to 0.25 floors/second. Note: the rate is NOT 4 seconds per floor! This is an extremely frequent error. **Always express rates as "distance over time,"** not as "time over distance."

The time is 2 minutes. The distance is unknown.

	R (floors/sec)	×	T (sec)	=	W (floors)
Elevator	0.25	×	120	=	?

Watch out! There is a problem with this RTD chart. The rate is expressed in floors per second, but the time is expressed in minutes. This will yield an incorrect answer.

To correct this table, we change the time into seconds. Then all the units will match.

Once the time has been converted from 2 minutes to 120 seconds, the time unit will match the rate unit, and we can solve for the distance using the $RT = D$ equation:

$$0.25(120) = d \qquad d = 30 \text{ floors}$$

Another example:

	R (km/hr)	×	T (hr)	=	W (km)
Train	90	×	?	=	450

> A train travels 90 kilometers/hr. How many hours does it take the train to travel 450,000 meters?

Before entering the information into the RTD chart, we convert the distance from 450,000 meters to 450 km. This matches the distance unit with the rate unit (kilometers per hour).

We can now solve for the time: $90t = 450$. Thus, $t = 5$ hours. Note that this time is the "stopwatch" time: if you started a stopwatch at the start of the trip, what would the stopwatch read at the end of the trip? This is not what a clock on the wall would read, but if you take the *difference* of the start and end clock times (say, 1 pm and 6 pm), you will get the stopwatch time of 5 hours.

The RTD chart may seem like overkill for relatively simple problems such as these. In fact, for such problems, you can simply set up the equation $RT = D$ or $RT = W$ and then substitute. However, the RTD chart comes into its own when we have more complicated scenarios that contain more than one RTD relationship, as we see in the next section.

*Manhattan*GRE*Prep
the new standard

Check Your Skills

1. Convert 10 meters per second to meters per hour.
2. It takes an inlet pipe 2 minutes to supply 30 gallons of water to a pool. How many hours will it take to fill a 27,000 gallon pool that starts out empty?

Answers can be found on page 59.

Multiple Rates Problems

Difficult GRE rate problems often involve rates, times, and distances for *more than one trip or traveler.* For instance, we might have more than one person taking a trip, or we might have one person making multiple trips. We expand the RTD chart by adding rows for each trip. Sometimes, we also add a third row, which may indicate a total.

	Rate (miles/hour)	×	Time (hour)	=	Distance (miles)
Trip 1		×		=	
Trip 2		×		=	
Total					

For each trip, the rate, time, and distance work in the usual manner ($RT = D$), but we have additional relationships among the multiple trips. Below is a list of typical relationships among the multiple trips or travelers.

RATE RELATIONS

Twice / half / n times as fast as

"Train A is traveling at twice the speed of Train B."

	Rate (miles/hour)	×	Time (hour)	=	Distance (miles)
Train A	$2r$	×		=	
Train B	r	×		=	

(Do not reverse these expressions!)

Slower / faster

"Wendy walks 1 mile per hour more slowly than Maurice."

	Rate (miles/hour)	×	Time (hour)	=	Distance (miles)
Wendy	$r - 1$	×		=	
Maurice	r	×		=	

Relative rates

	Rate (miles/hour)	×	Time (hour)	=	Distance (miles)
Car A	a	×		=	
Car B	b	×		=	
Shrinking Distance Between	$a + b$				

"Car A and Car B are driving directly <u>toward</u> each other."

For example, if Car A is going 30 miles per hour and Car B is going 40 miles per hour, then the distance between them is shrinking at a rate of 70 miles per hour. If the cars are driving <u>away</u> from each other, then the distance <u>grows</u> at a rate of $(a + b)$ miles per hour. Either way, the rates add up.

	Rate (miles/hour)	×	Time (hour)	=	Distance (miles)
Car A	a	×		=	
Car B	b	×		=	
Shrinking Distance Between	$a - b$				

"Car A is chasing Car B and catching up."

For example, if Car A is going 55 miles per hour, but Car B is going only 40 miles per hour, then Car A is <u>catching up</u> at 15 miles per hour—that is, the gap shrinks at that rate.

	Rate (miles/hour)	×	Time (hour)	=	Distance (miles)
Car A	a	×		=	
Car B	b	×		=	
Growing Distance Between	$b - a$				

"Car A is chasing Car B and falling behind."

TIME RELATIONS

Slower / faster

	Rate (meters/sec)	×	Time (sec)	=	Distance (meters)
Joey		×	$t - 30$	=	
Tommy		×	t	=	

"Joey runs a race 30 seconds faster than Tommy."

These signs are the *opposites* of the ones for the "slower / faster" rate relations. If Joey runs a race faster than Tommy, then Joey's speed is higher, but his time is lower.

Left … and met / arrived

> "Sue left her office at the same time as Tara left hers. They met some time later."

	Rate (miles/hour)	×	Time (hour)	=	Distance (miles)
Sue		×	t	=	
Tara		×	t	=	

Sue and Tara traveled for the same amount time.

> "Sue and Tara left at the same time, but Sue arrived home 1 hour before Tara did."

	Rate (miles/hour)	×	Time (hour)	=	Distance (miles)
Sue		×	$t - 1$	=	
Tara		×	t	=	

Sue traveled for 1 hour less than Tara.

> "Sue left the office 1 hour after Tara, but they met on the road."

	Rate (miles/hour)	×	Time (hour)	=	Distance (miles)
Sue		×	$t - 1$	=	
Tara		×	t	=	

Again, Sue traveled for 1 hour less than Tara.

A SAMPLE SITUATION

The numbers in the same row of an RTD table will always multiply across: Rate × Time _always_ equals Distance. However, the specifics of the problem determine _which columns_ (R, T, and/or D) _will add up into a total row._

The most common Multiple RTD situations are described below. Whenever you encounter a new Multiple RTD problem, try to make an analogy between the new problem and one of the following situations.

The "Kiss":

> "Car A and Car B start driving toward each other at the same time. Eventually they meet each other."

	Rate (miles/hour)	×	Time (hour)	=	Distance (miles)
Car A	a	×	t	=	A's distance
Car B	b	×	t	=	B's distance
Total	$a + b$		t		Total distance covered

ADD   SAME   ADD
(unless one car starts earlier than the other)

The "Quarrel": **Same math** as *"The Kiss"*.
> "Car A and Car B start driving <u>away</u> from each other at the same time…"

The "Chase":

	Rate (miles/hour)	×	Time (hour)	=	Distance (miles)
Car A	a	×	t	=	A's distance
Car B	b	×	t	=	B's distance
Relative Position	$a - b$		t		Change in the gap between the cars

> "Car A is chasing Car B. How long does it take for Car A to catch up to Car B?"

SUBTRACT   SAME   SUBTRACT
(unless one car starts earlier than the other)

The "Round Trip":

> "Jan drives from home to work in the morning, then takes the same route home in the evening."

	Rate (miles/hour)	×	Time (hour)	=	Distance (miles)
Going		×	time going	=	d
Return		×	time returning	=	d
Total			total time		$2d$

VARIES   ADD   ADD

We will address this specific scenario later, in the "Average Rate" section.

Often, you can make up a convenient value for the distance. Pick a Smart Number—a value that is a multiple of all the given rates or times.

The "Following footsteps":

> "Jan drives from home to the store along the same route as Bill."

	Rate (miles/hour)	×	Time (hour)	=	Distance (miles)
Jan		×		=	d
Bill		×		=	d

VARIES   VARIES   SAME

DISTANCE is the same for each person. Again, pick a Smart Number if necessary.

The "Hypothetical":

| "Jan drove home from work. If she had driven home along the same route 10 miles per hour faster…" |

	Rate (miles/hour)	×	Time (hour)	=	Distance (miles)
Actual	r	×		=	d
Hypothetical	$r + 10$	×		=	d
	VARIES		VARIES		SAME

No matter what situation exists in a problem, you will often have a choice as to how you name variables.

Use the following step-by-step method to solve Multiple RTD problems such as this:

> Stacy and Heather are 20 miles apart and walk towards each other along the same route. Stacy walks at a constant rate that is 1 mile per hour faster than Heather's constant rate of 5 miles/hour. If Heather starts her journey 24 minutes after Stacy, how far from her original destination has Heather walked when the two meet?
>
> (A) 7 miles (B) 8 miles (C) 9 miles (D) 10 miles (E) 12 miles

Make sure that you understand the physical situation portrayed in the problem. The category is "The Kiss": two people walk toward each other and meet. Notice that Stacy starts walking first. If necessary, you might even draw a picture to clarify the scene.

<u>First</u> convert any mismatched units. Because all the rates are given in miles per *hour*, you should convert the time that is given in *minutes*: $24 \min \times \dfrac{1 \text{ hr}}{60 \text{ min}} = 0.4$ hr.

<u>Second,</u> start setting up your RTD chart. Fill in all the numbers that you know or can compute very simply: Heather's speed is 5 miles/hour, and Stacy's speed is 5 + 1 = 6 miles/hour.

<u>Third,</u> try to introduce only one variable. If you introduce more than *one variable*, you will have to eliminate it later to solve the problem; this elimination can cost you valuable time. Let t stand for Heather's time. Also, we know that Stacy walked for 0.4 hours more than Heather, so Stacy's time is $t + 0.4$.

	Rate (mi/h)	×	Time (hr)	=	Distance (mi)
Stacy	6	×	$t + 0.4$	=	
Heather	5	×	t	=	
Total					20 mi

<u>Fourth,</u> complete the table by multiplying across rows (as always) and by adding the one column that can be added in this problem (which is <u>usually</u> distance, as it is in this case). (Because Stacy started walking earlier than Heather, you should <u>not</u> simply add the rates in this scenario. You can only add the rates for the period during which the women are <u>both</u> walking. More on this concept on the next page.)

	Rate (mi/h)	×	Time (hr)	=	Distance (mi)
Stacy	6	×	$t + 0.4$	=	$6t + 2.4$ mi
Heather	5	×	t	=	$5t$ mi
Total					20 mi

The table produces the equation $(6t + 2.4) + 5t = 20$, yielding $t = 1.6$. Heather's distance is therefore $5t$, or 8 miles.

Finally, notice that _if you were stuck,_ you could have eliminated some wrong answer choices by thinking about the physical situation. Heather started later and walked more slowly; therefore, she cannot have covered half the 20 miles before Stacy reached her. Thus, Choices D (10 miles) and E (12 miles) are impossible.

ALTERNATE APPROACH: RELATIVE RATES

You can simplify this problem by thinking further about "The Kiss" problem above. First, find the distance Stacy walks in the first 24 minutes (= 0.4 hours) by herself: $d = r \times t = (6 \text{ mi/h}) \times (0.4 \text{ h}) = 2.4$ mi. Therefore, once Heather starts walking, the two women have $20 - 2.4 = 17.6$ miles left to travel. Because the two women are now traveling for the _same time_ in _opposite directions_ (in this case, toward each other), you can just use the concept of relative rate: the distance between them is shrinking at the rate of $6 + 5 = 11$ miles per hour.

This idea of relative rates eliminates the need for two separate equations, leading to the simplified table shown to the right. Solving the resulting equation gives $t = 1.6$ hours. This is the time during which both women are walking.

R (mi/hr)	×	T (hr)	=	D (mi)
11	×	t	=	17.6

Now set up another _simple_ RTD table for Heather by herself.

Heather's distance is therefore $5 \times 1.6 = 8$ miles.

R (mi/hr)	×	T (hr)	=	D (mi)
5	×	1.6	=	D

The algebraic manipulations are actually very similar in both solutions, but the second approach is more intuitive, and the intermediate calculations make sense. By reformulating problems, you can often increase your understanding and your confidence, even if you do not save that much algebraic work.

Check Your Skills

3. One hour after Adrienne started walking the 60 miles from X to Y, James started walking from X to Y as well. Adrienne walks 3 miles per hour, and James walks 1 mile per hour faster than Adrienne. How far from X will James be when he catches up to Adrienne?

(A) 8 miles (B) 9 miles (C) 10 miles (D) 11 miles (E) 12 miles

4. Nicky and Cristina are running a 1,000 meter race. Since Cristina is faster than Nicky, she gives him a 12 second head start. If Cristina runs at a pace of 5 meters per second and Nicky runs at a pace of only 3 meters per second, how many seconds will Nicky have run before Cristina catches up to him?

(A) 15 seconds (B) 18 seconds (C) 25 seconds (D) 30 seconds (E) 45 seconds

Answer can be found on pages 59–60.

ManhattanGRE Prep
the new standard

Average Rate: Don't Just Add and Divide

Consider the following problem:

> If Lucy walks to work at a rate of 4 miles per hour, but she walks home by the same route at a rate of 6 miles per hour, what is Lucy's average walking rate for the round trip?

It is very tempting to find an average rate as you would find any other average: add and divide. Thus, you might say that Lucy's average rate is 5 miles per hour ($4 + 6 = 10$ and $10 \div 2 = 5$). However, this is INCORRECT!

If an object moves the **same distance** twice, but at **different rates**, then *the average rate will NEVER be the average of the two rates given for the two legs of the journey*. In fact, because the object spends <u>more time</u> traveling at the slower rate, *the average rate will be closer to the slower of the two rates than to the faster.*

In order to find the average rate, you must first find the TOTAL combined time for the trips and the TOTAL combined distance for the trips.

First, we need a value for the distance. Since all we need to know to determine the average rate is the *total time* and *total distance*, we can actually pick any number for the distance. The portion of the total distance represented by each part of the trip ("Going" and "Return") will dictate the time.

Pick a Smart Number for the distance. Since you would like to choose a multiple of the two rates in the problem, 4 and 6, 12 is an ideal choice.

Set up a Multiple RTD Chart:

	Rate (mi/hr)	×	Time (hr)	=	Distance (mi)
Going	4 mi/hr	×		=	12 mi
Return	6 mi/hr	×		=	12 mi
Total	?	×		=	24 mi

The times can be found using the *RTD* equation. For the GOING trip, $4t = 12$, so $t = 3$ hrs. For the RETURN trip, $6t = 12$, so $t = 2$ hrs. Thus, the total time is 5 hrs.

	Rate (mi/hr)	×	Time (hr)	=	Distance (mi)
Going	4 mi/hr	×	**3 hrs**	=	12 mi
Return	6 mi/hr	×	**2 hrs**	=	12 mi
Total	?	×	**5 hrs**	=	24 mi

Now that we have the total Time and the total Distance, we can find the Average Rate using the RTD formula:

$RT = D$
$r(5) = 24$
$r = 4.8$ miles per hour

Again, 4.8 miles per hour is *not* the simple average of 4 miles per hour and 6 miles per hour. In fact, it is the weighted average of the two rates, with the *times* as the weights. Because of that, the average rate is closer to the slower of the two rates.

You can test different numbers for the distance (try 24 or 36) to prove that you will get the same answer, regardless of the number you choose for the distance.

Check Your Skills

5. Juan bikes halfway to school at 9 miles per hour, and walks the rest of the distance at 3 miles per hour. What is Juan's average speed for the whole trip?

Answer can be found on page 60.

Work Problems

Work problems are just another type of rate problem. Just like all other rate problems, work problems involve three elements: rate, time, and "distance."

WORK: In work problems, distance is replaced by work, or <u>output</u>, which refers to the number of jobs completed or the number of items produced.

TIME: This is the time spent working.

RATE: In motion problems, the rate is a ratio of distance to time, or the amount of distance traveled in one time unit. In work problems, the rate is a ratio of <u>work</u> to <u>time</u>, or the amount of <u>work completed</u> in <u>one time unit.</u>

Figuring Work Rates

Work rates usually include one major twist not seen in distance problems: you often have to *calculate* the work rate.

In distance problems, if the rate (speed) is known, it will normally be *given* to you as a ready-to-use number. In work problems, though, you will usually have to *figure out* the rate from some given information about how many jobs the agent can complete in a given amount of time:

$$\text{Work rate} = \frac{\text{Given \# of jobs}}{\text{Given amount of time}}, \text{ or } \frac{1}{\text{Time to complete 1 job}}$$

For instance, if Oscar can perform one hand surgery in 1.5 hours, his work rate is given by:

$$\frac{1 \text{ operation}}{1.5 \text{ hours}} = \frac{2}{3} \text{ operation per hour}$$

Remember the rate is NOT 1.5 hours per hand surgery! **Always express work rates as <u>jobs</u> per <u>unit time,</u> not as time per job.** Also, you need to distinguish this type of general information—which is meant to specify the work <u>rate</u>—from the data given about the actual work performed, or the time required to perform that specific work.

For example:

> If a copier can make 3 copies every 2 seconds, how long will it take to make 40 copies?

Here, the work is 40 copies, because this is the number of items that will be produced. The time is unknown. The rate is 3 copies/2 seconds, or 1.5 copies per second. Notice the use of the verb "can" with the general rate.

> If it takes Anne 5 hours to paint one fence, and she has been working for 7 hours, how many fences has she painted?

Here the time is 7 hours, because that is the time which Anne spent working. The work done is unknown. Anne's general working rate is 1 fence per 5 hours, or 1/5 fence per hour. Be careful: her rate is not 5 hours per fence, but rather 0.2 fences per hour. Again, always express rates as <u>work per time unit</u>, not time per work unit. Also, notice that the "5 hours" is part of the general rate, whereas the "7 hours" is the actual time for this specific situation. Distinguish the general description of the work rate from the specific description of the episode or task. Here is a useful test: you should be able to add the phrase "in general" to the rate information. For example, we can easily imagine the following:

> If, <u>in general</u>, a copier can make 3 copies every 2 seconds…

> If, <u>in general</u>, it takes Anne 5 hours to paint one fence…

Since the insertion of "in general" makes sense, we know that these parts of the problem contain the general rate information.

Basic work problems are solved like basic rate problems, using an RTW chart or the RTW equation. Simply replace the distance with the work. They can also be solved with a simple proportion. Here are both methods for Anne's work problem:

| **RTW CHART** | | **PROPORTION** |

$$\begin{array}{ccccc} R & \times & T & = & W \\ \text{(fence/hr)} & & \text{(hr)} & & \text{(fences)} \\ \hline \dfrac{1/5}{\text{fence/hr}} & \times & 7 \text{ hours} & = & x \end{array}$$

$$\frac{5 \text{ hours}}{1 \text{ fence}} = \frac{7 \text{ hours}}{x \text{ fences}}$$

$$RT = W$$

$$5x = 7$$

$$\frac{1}{5}(7) = \frac{7}{5}$$

$$x = \frac{7}{5}$$

Anne has painted 7/5 of a fence, or 1.4 fences. Note that you can set up the proportion either as "hours/fence" or as "fences/hour." You must simply be consistent on both sides of the equation. However, any rate in an $RT = W$ relationship must be in "fences/hour." (Verify for yourself that the answer to the copier problem above is 80/3 seconds or 26 2/3 seconds.)

COMBINED WORK PROBLEMS

Sometimes multiple entities (workers, machines, etc.) work <u>together</u> to complete jobs. By always expressing work rates as jobs per unit of time, we can <u>add</u> the work rates for the multiple entities that are working together.

Check Your Skills

6. Sophie can address 20 envelopes in one hour. How long will it take her to address 50 envelopes?

7. If a steel mill can produce 1500 feet of I-beams every 20 minutes, how many feet of I-beams can it produce in 50 minutes?

8. John can complete a job in 12 minutes. If Andy helps John, they can complete the job in 4 minutes. How long would it take for Andy to complete the job on his own?

Answers can be found on page 60.

Population Problems

The final type of rate problem on the GRE is the population problem. In such problems, some population typically increases <u>by a common factor</u> every time period. These can be solved with a Population Chart.

Consider the following example:

> The population of a certain type of bacterium triples every 10 minutes. If the population of a colony 20 minutes ago was 100, in approximately how many minutes from now will the bacteria population reach 24,000?

You can solve simple population problems, such as this one, by using a Population Chart. Make a table with a few rows, labeling one of the middle rows as "NOW." Work forward, backward, or both (as necessary in the problem), obeying any conditions given in the problem statement about the rate of growth or decay. In this case, simply triple each population number as you move down a row. Notice that while the population increases by a constant <u>factor</u>, it does <u>not</u> increase by a constant <u>amount</u> each time period.

For this problem, the Population Chart below shows that the bacterial population will reach 24,000 about 30 minutes from now.

In some cases, you might pick a Smart Number for a starting point in your Population Chart. If you do so, pick a number that makes the computations as simple as possible.

Time Elapsed	Population
20 minutes ago	100
10 minutes ago	300
NOW	900
in 10 minutes	2,700
in 20 minutes	8,100
in 30 minutes	24,300

Check Your Skills

9. The population of amoebas in a colony doubles every two days. If there were 200 amoebas in the colony six days ago, how many amoebas will there be four days from now?

Answer can be found on page 61.

Check Your Skills Answers

1. **36,000 meters/hour:** First convert seconds to minutes. There are 60 seconds in a minute, so 10 m/sec × 60 = 600 m/min.

Now convert minutes to hours. There are 60 minutes in 1 hour, so 600 m/min × 60 = 36,000 m/hr.

2. **30 hours:** First simplify the rate. $R = \dfrac{30 \text{ gal}}{2 \text{ min}} = \dfrac{15 \text{ gal}}{1 \text{ min}}$, which is the same as 15 gal/min. The question asks for the number of hours it will take to fill the pool, so convert minutes to hours. There are 60 minutes in an hour, so the rate is 15 gal/min × 60 = 900 gal/hr. Now we can set up an RTW chart. Let t be the time it takes to fill the pool.

	R (gal/hr)	×	T (hr)	=	W (gallons)
inlet pipe	900	×	t	=	27,000

$900t = 27{,}000$
$t = 30$ hours

3. **12 miles:** Organize this information in an RTD chart as follows:

	R (mi/hr)	×	T (hr)	=	D (mi)
Adrienne	3	×	t + 1	=	d
James	4	×	t	=	d
Total	—				2d

Set up algebraic equations to relate the information in the chart, using the $RT = D$ equation.

ADRIENNE: $3(t + 1) = d$
JAMES: $4t = d$

Substitute $4t$ for d in the first equation: $3(t + 1) = 4t$
$3t + 3 = 4t$
$t = 3$

Therefore, $d = 4(3) = 12$ miles.

Alternatively, you can model this problem as a "Chase." Adrienne has a 3-mile headstart on James (since Adrienne started walking 1 hour before James, and Adrienne's speed is 3 miles per hour). Since James is walking 1 mile per hour faster than Adrienne, it will take 3 hours for him to catch up to Adrienne. Therefore, he will have walked (4 miles per hour)(3 hours) = 12 miles by the time he catches up to Adrienne.

4. **30 seconds:** This is a "Chase" problem in which the people are moving in the SAME DIRECTION.

Fill in the RTD chart. Note that Nicky starts 12 seconds before Cristina, so Nicky's time is $t + 12$.

Write expressions for the total distance, and then set these two distances equal to each other.

	R (m/s)	×	T (second)	=	D (meter)
Cristina	5	×	t	=	5t
Nicky	3	×	t + 12	=	3(t + 12)

CRISTINA: $5t$ = distance
NICKY: $3(t + 12)$ = distance
COMBINE: $5t = 3(t + 12)$
                     $5t = 3t + 36$
                     $2t = 36$
                     $t = 18$

Therefore, Nicky will have run for $18 + 12 = 30$ seconds before Cristina catches up to him.

5. **4.5 mph:** Assume a Smart Number for the distance to school. The Smart number should be divisible by 9 and 3. The simplest choice is 9 miles for this distance.

Time biking: $T = D/R = 9/9 = 1$ hr
Time walking: $T = D/R = 9/3 = 3$ hr
Total Time: 1 hr + 3 hr = 4 hr

$$\text{Average Speed} = \frac{\text{Total Distance}}{\text{Total Time}} = \frac{18 \text{ miles}}{4 \text{ hours}} = 4.5 \text{ mph}$$

6. **2.5 hours:** If she addresses 20 envelopes in 1 hour, then the rate at which she addresses is 20 envelopes/hr. We can set up an RTW equation.

20 envelopes/hr $\times T$ = 50 envelopes
$T = 50/20 = 2.5$ hr

7. **3,750 feet:** The rate at which the steel mill produces I-beams is $\dfrac{1500 \text{ ft}}{20 \text{ min}} = 75$ ft/min. We can set up an *RTW* equation. Let w represent the number of feet of I-beam produced:

75 ft/min $\times$ 50 min = w
3,750 ft = w

8. **6 minutes:** Always express work rates as jobs per unit of time. In so doing, the combined rates for John and Andy are additive:

$$\underbrace{\frac{1 \text{ job}}{12 \text{ minutes}}}_{\text{John}} + \underbrace{\frac{1 \text{ job}}{a \text{ minutes}}}_{\text{Andy}} = \frac{1 \text{ job}}{4 \text{ minutes}}$$

$$\frac{1}{a} = \frac{3}{12} - \frac{1}{12} = \frac{1}{6} \qquad a = 6 \text{ minutes}$$

9. **6,400:**

Time	Population
6 days ago	200
4 days ago *(Careful! Count by two days.)*	400
2 days ago	800
NOW	1,600
2 days from now	3,200
4 days from now	6,400

Problem Set

Solve the following problems, using the strategies you have learned in this section. Use RTD or RTW charts as appropriate to organize information.

1.   A cat travels at a speed of 60 inches/second. How long will it take this cat to travel 300 feet? (12 inches = 1 foot)

2.   Water is being poured into a tank at the rate of approximately 4 cubic feet per hour. If the tank is 6 feet long, 4 feet wide, and 8 feet deep, how many hours will it take to fill up the tank?

3.   The population of grasshoppers doubles in a particular field every year. Approximately how many years will it take the population to grow from 2,000 grasshoppers to 1,000,000 or more?

4.   An empty bucket being filled with paint at a constant rate takes 6 minutes to be filled to 7/10 of its capacity. How much more time will it take to fill the bucket to full capacity?

5.   4 years from now, the population of a colony of bees will reach 1.6×10^8. If the population of the colony doubles every 2 years, what was the population 4 years ago?

6.   The Technotronic can produce 5 bad songs per hour. Wanting to produce bad songs more quickly, the record label also buys a Wonder Wheel, which works as fast as the Technotronic. Working together, how many bad songs can the two produce in 72 minutes?

7.   Jack is putting together gift boxes at a rate of 3 per hour in the first hour. Then Jill comes over and yells, "Work faster!" Jack, now nervous, works at the rate of only 2 gift boxes per hour for the next 2 hours. Then Alexandra comes to Jack and whispers, "The steadiest hand is capable of the divine." Jack, calmer, then puts together 5 gift boxes in the fourth hour. What is the average rate at which Jack puts together gift boxes over the entire period?

8.   A bullet train leaves Kyoto for Tokyo traveling 240 miles per hour at 12 noon. Ten minutes later, a train leaves Tokyo for Kyoto traveling 160 miles per hour. If Tokyo and Kyoto are 300 miles apart, at what time will the trains pass each other?

     (A) 12:40 pm   (B) 12:49 pm   (C) 12:55 pm   (D) 1:00 pm   (E) 1:05 pm

9.   Andrew drove from A to B at 60 miles per hour. Then he realized that he forgot something at A, and drove back at 80 miles per hour. He then zipped back to B at 90 mph. What was his approximate average speed in miles per hour for the entire trip?

10. A car travels from Town A to Town B at an average speed of 40 miles per hour, and returns immediately along the same route at an average speed of 50 miles per hour. What is the average speed in miles per hour for the round-trip?

11. Two hoses are pouring water into an empty pool. Hose 1 alone would fill up the pool in 6 hours. Hose 2 alone would fill up the pool in 4 hours. How long would it take for both hoses to fill up two-thirds of the pool?

12. Amy takes 6 minutes to pack a box and Brianna takes 5 minutes to pack a box. How many <u>hours</u> will it take them to pack 110 boxes?

13.

Hector can solve one word
problem every 4 minutes
before noon, and one word
problem every 10 minutes
after noon.

Quantity A

The number of word problems
Hector can solve between
11:40am and noon

Quantity B

The number of word
problems Hector can solve
between noon and 12:40pm

14.

The number of users (non-zero)
of a social networking website
doubles every 4 months.

Quantity A

Ten times the number of users
one year ago

Quantity B

The number of users today

15.

A bullet train can cover the
420 kilometers between Xenia
and York at a rate of
240 kilometers per hour.

Quantity A

The number of minutes it will take
the train to travel from Xenia to York

Quantity B

110

1. **1 minute:** This is a simple application of the $RT = D$ formula, involving one unit conversion. First convert the rate, 60 inches/second, into 5 feet/second (given that 12 inches = 1 foot). Substitute this value for R. Substitute the distance, 300 feet, for D. Then solve:

$$(5 \text{ ft/s})(t) = 300 \text{ ft}$$

$$t = \frac{300 \text{ ft}}{5 \text{ ft/s}} = 60 \text{ seconds} = 1 \text{ minute}$$

R (ft/sec)	$\times$	T (sec)	$=$	D (ft)
5	$\times$	t	$=$	300

2. **48 hours:** The capacity of the tank is $6 \times 4 \times 8$, or 192 cubic feet. Use the $RT = W$ equation, substituting the rate, 4 ft³/hour, for R, and the capacity, 192 cubic feet, for W:

$$(4 \text{ cubic feet/hr})(t) = 192 \text{ cubic feet}$$

$$t = \frac{192 \text{ cubic feet}}{4 \text{ cubic feet/hr}} = 48 \text{ hours}$$

R (ft³/hr)	$\times$	T (hr)	$=$	W (ft)
4	$\times$	t	$=$	192

3. **9 years:** Organize the information given in a population chart. Notice that since the population is increasing exponentially, it does not take very long for the population to top 1,000,000.

Time Elapsed	Population
NOW	2,000
1 year	4,000
2 years	8,000
3 years	16,000
4 years	32,000
5 years	64,000
6 years	128,000
7 years	256,000
8 years	512,000
9 years	1,024,000

4. **$2\frac{4}{7}$ minutes:** Use the $RT = W$ equation to solve for the rate, with $t = 6$ minutes and $w = 7/10$.

$$r(6 \text{ minutes}) = 7/10$$

$$r = 7/10 \div 6 = \frac{7}{10} \text{ buckets per minute.}$$

R (bkt/min)	$\times$	T (min)	$=$	W (bucket)
r	$\times$	6	$=$	7/10

Then, substitute this rate into the equation again, using 3/10 for w (the remaining work to be done).

$$\left(\frac{7}{60}\right)t = \frac{3}{10}$$

$$t = \frac{3}{10} \div \frac{7}{60} = \frac{18}{7} = 2\frac{4}{7} \text{ minutes}$$

R Regular	$\times$	T Regular	$=$	W Regular
7/60	$\times$	t	$=$	3/10

5. **1×10^7:** Organize the information given in a population chart.

Then, convert:

$$0.1 \times 10^8 = 10,000,000 = 1 \times 10^7 \text{ bees.}$$

Time Elapsed	Population
4 years ago	0.1×10^8
2 years ago	0.2×10^8
NOW	0.4×10^8
in 2 years	0.8×10^8
in 4 years	1.6×10^8

6. **12 songs:** Since this is a "working together" problem, add the individual rates: 5 + 5 = 10 songs per hour.

The two machines together can produce 10 bad songs in 1 hour. Convert the given time into hours:

$$(72 \text{ minutes})\left(\frac{1 \text{ hour}}{60 \text{ minutes}}\right) = \frac{72}{60} = 1.2 \text{ hours}$$

Then, use the $RT = W$ equation to find the total work done:

$(10)(1.2 \text{ hours}) = w$
$w = 12$ bad songs

	R (songs/hr)	×	T (hr)	=	W (songs)
	10	×	1.2	=	w

7. **3 boxes per hour:** The average rate is equal to the total work done divided by the time in which the work was done. Remember that you cannot simply average the rates. You must find the total work and total time. The total time is 4 hours. To find the total work, add up the boxes Jack put together in each hour: 3 + 2 + 2 + 5 = 12. Therefore, the average rate is $\frac{12}{4}$, or 3 boxes per hour. The completed chart looks like the one to the right:

	R (box/hr)	×	T (hr)	=	W (box)
Phase 1	3	×	1	=	3
Phase 2	2	×	2	=	4
Phase 3	5	×	1	=	5
Total	3 = 12/4		4 Sum		12 Sum

8. **12:49 P.M.:** This is a "Kiss" problem in which the trains are moving TOWARDS each other.

Solve this problem by filling in the RTD chart. Note that the train going from Kyoto to Tokyo leaves first, so its time is longer by 10 minutes, which is 1/6 hour.

Next, write the expressions for the distance that each train travels, in terms of t. Now, sum those distances and set that total equal to 300 miles.

	R (mi/hr)	×	T (hr)	=	D (mi)
Train K to T	240	×	$t + 1/6$	=	$240(t + 1/6)$
Train T to K	160	×	t	=	$160t$
Total	—		—		300

$$240\left(t + \frac{1}{6}\right) + 160t = 300$$

$$240t + 40 + 160t = 300$$
$$400t = 260$$
$$20t = 13$$
$$t = \frac{13}{20} \text{ hour} = \frac{39}{60} \text{ hour} = 39 \text{ minutes}$$

The first train leaves at 12 noon. The second train leaves at 12:10 P.M. Thirty-nine minutes after the second train has left, at 12:49 P.M., the trains pass each other.

9. **Approximately 74.5 mph:** Use a Multiple RTD chart to solve this problem. Start by selecting a Smart Number for d: 720 miles. (This is a common multiple of the 3 rates in the problem.) Then, work backwards to find the time for each trip and the total time:

$$t_A = \frac{720}{60} = 12 \text{ hrs}$$

$$t_B = \frac{720}{80} = 9 \text{ hrs}$$

$$t_C = \frac{720}{90} = 8 \text{ hrs}$$

	R (mi/hr)	×	T (hr)	=	D (mi)
A to B	60	×	t_A	=	720
B to A	80	×	t_B	=	720
A to B	90	×	t_C	=	720
Total	—		t		2,160

$$t = 12 + 9 + 8 = 29 \text{ hours}$$

The average speed $= \dfrac{\text{total distance}}{\text{total time}} = \dfrac{2{,}160}{29} \approx 74.5$ miles per hour.

10. $44\frac{4}{9}$ **miles per hour**. Use a Multiple RTD chart to solve this problem. Start by selecting a Smart Number for d: 200 miles. (This is a common multiple of the 2 rates in the problem.) Then, work backwards to find the time for each trip and the total time:

$$t_1 = \frac{200}{40} = 5 \text{ hrs} \qquad\qquad t_2 = \frac{200}{50} = 4 \text{ hrs} \qquad\qquad t = 4 + 5 = 9 \text{ hours}$$

The average speed $= \dfrac{\text{total distance}}{\text{total time}} = \dfrac{400}{9} = 44\frac{4}{9}$ miles per hour.

Do NOT simply average 40 miles per hour and 50 miles per hour to get 45 miles per hour. The fact that the right answer is very close to this wrong result makes this error especially pernicious: avoid it at all costs!

11. $1\frac{3}{5}$ **hours :** If Hose 1 can fill the pool in 6 hours, its rate is 1/6 pool per hour, or the fraction of the job it can do in one hour. Likewise, if Hose 2 can fill the pool in 4 hours, its rate is 1/4 pool per hour. Therefore, the combined rate is 5/12 pool per hour (1/4 + 1/6 = 5/12).

$RT = W$
$(5/12)t = 2/3$

	R (pool/hr)	×	T (hr)	=	W (pool)
	5/12	×	t	=	2/3

$$t = \frac{2}{\cancel{3}_1} \times \frac{\cancel{12}^{4}}{5} = \frac{8}{5} = 1\frac{3}{5}$$

12. **5 hours:** Working together, Amy and Brianna pack $\dfrac{1}{6} + \dfrac{1}{5} = \dfrac{11}{30}$ boxes per minute. Using a proportion:

$$\frac{11 \text{ boxes}}{30 \text{ minutes}} = \frac{110 \text{ boxes}}{x \text{ minutes}}$$

$$x = \frac{(110)(30)}{(11)} = 300 \text{ minutes, or 5 hours.}$$

13. **A:** This problem can be solved by an RTW chart or by a proportion. There are 20 minutes between 11:40am and noon, and 40 minutes between noon and 12:40pm. Hector's work rate is different for the two time periods. For the work period before noon, this is the proportion:

Let *b* represent the number of problems Hector solves *before* noon:

$$\frac{b}{20 \text{ min}} = \frac{1 \text{ problem}}{4 \text{ min}}$$

$$4b = 20$$
$$b = 5$$

Let *a* represent the number of problems Hector solves *after* noon. The proportion can be written like this:

$$\frac{a}{40 \text{ min}} = \frac{1 \text{ problem}}{10 \text{ min}}$$

$$10a = 40$$

$$a = 4$$

Rewrite the quantities:

<table>
<tr><td align="center"><u>**Quantity A**</u></td><td align="center"><u>**Quantity B**</u></td></tr>
<tr><td align="center">The number of word problems
Hector can solve between 11:40am
and noon = **5**</td><td align="center">The number of word problems
Hector can solve between noon
and 12:40pm = **4**</td></tr>
</table>

Therefore, **Quantity A is greater.**

14. **A:** Set up a population chart, letting *X* denote the number of users one year ago:

Time	Number of users
12 months ago	X
8 months ago	$2X$
4 months ago	$4X$
NOW	$8X$

10 times the number of users one year ago is $10X$, while the number of users today is $8X$. Rewrite the quantities:

Quantity A	**Quantity B**
Ten times the number of users one year ago = $10X$	The number of users today = $8X$

$10X$ is greater than $8X$ because X must be a positive number. Thus **Quantity A is greater.**

15 **B:** We can use the rate equation to solve for the time it will take the train to cover the distance. Our answer will be in hours because the given rate is in kilometers per hour. Let t stand for the total time of the trip.

$$R \times T = D$$

$$(240) \times t = (420)$$

$$t = \frac{420}{240} = \frac{7}{4}$$

(Note that we can omit the units in our calculation if we verify ahead of time that we are dealing with a consistent system of units.) Finally, we need to convert the time from hours into minutes: multiply $\frac{7}{4}$ by 60:

$$\frac{7}{4} \times 60 = \frac{7}{\cancel{4}} \times \cancel{60}^{15} = 105 \text{ minutes}$$

Rewrite the quantities:

Quantity A	**Quantity B**
The number of minutes it will take the train to travel from Xenia to York = **105**	**110**

Alternately, you can use the value in Quantity B. Assume the train traveled for 110 minutes. Convert 110 minutes to hours:

$$\frac{110}{60} = \frac{11}{6} \text{ hours}$$

Now multiply the time ($\frac{11}{6}$ hours) by the rate (240 kilometers per hour) to calculate the distance.

$$D = \frac{11}{6} \times 240 = \frac{11}{\cancel{6}} \times \cancel{240}^{40} = 440 \text{ kilometers}$$

The train can travel 440 kilometers in 110 minutes, but the distance between the cities is 420 kilometers. Therefore, the train must have traveled less than 110 minutes to reach its destination.

Therefore **Quantity B is greater.**

g

Chapter 4
of
WORD PROBLEMS

RATIOS

In This Chapter . . .

- Label Each Part of the Ratio with Units

- Proportions

- The Unknown Multiplier

- Multiple Ratios: Make a Common Term

RATIOS

A ratio expresses a particular relationship between two or more quantities. Here are some examples of ratios:

The two partners spend time working in the ratio of 1 to 3. For every 1 hour the first partner works, the second partner works 3 hours.

Three sisters invest in a certain stock in the ratio of 2 to 3 to 8. For every $2 the first sister invests, the second sister invests $3, and the third sister invests $8.

The ratio of men to women in the room is 3 to 4. For every 3 men, there are 4 women.

Here are some key points about ratios:

Ratios can be expressed in different ways:

(1) Using the word "to," as in 3 to 4

(2) Using a colon, as in 3 : 4

(3) By writing a fraction, as in $\dfrac{3}{4}$ (note that this only works for ratios of exactly <u>2</u> quantities)

Ratios can express a part-part relationship or a part-whole relationship:

A part–part relationship: The ratio of men to women in the office is 3:4.
A part–whole relationship: There are 3 men for every 7 employees.

Notice that if there are only two parts in the whole, you can derive a part–whole ratio from a part–part ratio, and vice versa.

The relationship that ratios express is division:

If the ratio of men to women in the office is 3 : 4, then the number of men *divided by* the number of women equals $\dfrac{3}{4}$ or 0.75.

Remember that ratios only express a *relationship* between two or more items; they do not provide enough information, on their own, to determine the exact quantity for each item. For example, knowing that the ratio of men to women in an office is 3 to 4 does NOT tell us exactly how many men and how many women are in the office. All we know is that the number of men is $\dfrac{3}{4}$ the number of women.

If two quantities have a **constant ratio**, they are in direct proportion to each other.

If the ratio of men to women in the office is 3 : 4, then $\dfrac{\text{\# of men}}{\text{\# of women}} = \dfrac{3}{4}$.

If the number of men is directly proportional to the number of women, then the number of men divided by the number of women is some constant.

Label Each Part of the Ratio with Units

The order in which a ratio is given is vital. For example, "the ratio of dogs to cats is 2 : 3" is very different from "the ratio of dogs to cats is 3 : 2." The first ratio says that for every 2 dogs, there are 3 cats. The second ratio says that for every 3 dogs, there are 2 cats.

It is very easy to accidentally reverse the order of a ratio—especially on a timed test like the GRE. Therefore, to avoid these reversals, always _write units_ on either the ratio itself or the variables you create, or both.

Thus, if the ratio of dogs to cats is 2 : 3, you can write $\dfrac{x \text{ dogs}}{y \text{ cats}} = \dfrac{2 \text{ dogs}}{3 \text{ cats}}$, or simply $\dfrac{x \text{ dogs}}{y \text{ cats}} = \dfrac{2}{3}$, or even $\dfrac{D}{C} = \dfrac{2 \text{ dogs}}{3 \text{ cats}}$,

where D and C are variables standing for the number of dogs and cats, respectively.

However, do not just write $\dfrac{x}{y} = \dfrac{2}{3}$. You could easily forget which variable stands for cats and which for dogs.

Also, NEVER write $\dfrac{2d}{3c}$. The reason is that you might think that d and c stand for _variables_—that is, numbers in their own right. Always write the full unit out.

Proportions

Simple ratio problems can be solved with a proportion.

> The ratio of girls to boys in the class is 4 to 7. If there are 35 boys in the class, how many girls are there?

Step 1: Set up a labeled PROPORTION:

$$\frac{4 \text{ girls}}{7 \text{ boys}} = \frac{x \text{ girls}}{35 \text{ boys}}$$

Step 2: Cross-multiply to solve:
$$140 = 7x$$
$$x = 20$$

To save time, you should cancel factors out of proportions before cross-multiplying. You can cancel factors either vertically within a fraction or horizontally across an equals sign:

$$\frac{4 \text{ girls}}{7 \text{ boys}} = \frac{x \text{ girls}}{35 \text{ boys}} \qquad \frac{4 \text{ girls}}{\cancel{7} \, 1 \text{ boy}} = \frac{x \text{ girls}}{\cancel{35} \, 5 \text{ boys}} \qquad \frac{4}{1} = \frac{x}{5} \qquad x = 20$$

**Note: never cancel factors diagonally across an equals sign.** That would change the values incorrectly.

Check Your Skills

1. The ratio of apples to oranges in a fruit basket is 3:5. If there are 15 apples, how many oranges are there?
2. Mike has 7 jazz CDs for every 12 classical CDs in his collection. If he has 60 classical CDs, how many jazz CDs does he have?

Answers can be found on page 77.

The Unknown Multiplier

For more complicated ratio problems, in which the total of <u>all</u> items is given, the "Unknown Multiplier" technique is useful.

> The ratio of men to women in a room is 3 : 4. If there are 56 people in the room, how many of the people are men?

Using the methods from the previous page, you can write the ratio relationship as $\dfrac{M \text{ men}}{W \text{ women}} = \dfrac{3}{4}$. Together with $M + W = \text{Total} = 56$, you can solve for M (and W, for that matter). The algebra for these "two equations and two unknowns" is not too difficult.

However, there is even an easier way. It requires a slight shift in your thinking, but if you can make this shift, <u>*you can save yourself a lot of work on some problems.*</u> Instead of representing the number of men as M, represent it as $3x$, where x is some unknown (positive) number. Likewise, instead of representing the number of women as W, represent it as $4x$, where x is the same unknown number. In this case (as in many others), x has to be a whole number. This is another example of a hidden constraint.

What does this seemingly odd step accomplish? It guarantees that the ratio of men to women is 3 : 4. The ratio of men to women can now be expressed as $\dfrac{3x}{4x}$, which reduces to $\dfrac{3}{4}$, the desired ratio. (Note that we can cancel the x's because we know that x is not zero.) This variable x is known as the Unknown Multiplier. The Unknown Multiplier allows us to reduce the number of variables, making the algebra easier.

Now determine the value of the Unknown Multiplier, using the other equation.

$$\text{Men} + \text{Women} = \text{Total} = 56$$

$$3x + 4x = 56$$

$$7x = 56$$

$$x = 8$$

Now we know that the value of x, the Unknown Multiplier, is 8. Therefore, we can determine the exact number of men and women in the room:

> The number of men = $3x = 3(8) = 24$. The number of women = $4x = 4(8) = 32$.

When *can* you use the Unknown Multiplier? You can use it ONCE per problem. Every other ratio in the problem must be set up with a proportion using the already defined unknown multiplier. **You should never have two Unknown Multipliers in the same problem.**

When *should* you use the Unknown Multiplier? You should use it when (a) the <u>total</u> items is given, or (b) neither quantity in the ratio is already equal to a number or a variable expression. Generally, the first ratio in a problem can be set up with an Unknown Multiplier. In the "girls & boys" problem on the previous page, however, we can glance ahead and see that the number of boys is given as 35. This means that we can just set up a simple proportion to solve the problem.

The Unknown Multiplier is particularly useful with three-part ratios:

> A recipe calls for amounts of lemon juice, wine, and water in the ratio of
> 2 : 5 : 7. If all three combined yield 35 milliliters of liquid, how much wine was included?

Make a quick table:

$$\text{Lemon Juice} + \text{Wine} + \text{Water} = \text{Total}$$
$$2x + 5x + 7x = 14x$$

Now solve: $14x = 35$, or $x = 2.5$. Thus, the amount of wine is $5x = 5(2.5) = 12.5$ milliliters.

In this problem, the Unknown Multiplier turns out not to be an integer. This result is fine, because the problem deals with continuous quantities (milliliters of liquids). In problems like the first one, which deals with integer quantities (men and women), the Unknown Multipier must be a positive integer. In that specific problem, the multiplier is <u>literally the number of "complete sets" of 3 men and 4 women each.</u>

Check Your Skills

3. The ratio of apples to oranges in a fruit basket is 3:5. If there are a total of 48 fruit, how many oranges are there?
4. Steve has nuts, bolts and washers in the ratio 5:4:6. If he has a total of 180 pieces of hardware, how many bolts does he have?
5. A dry mixture consists of 3 cups of flour for every 2 cups of sugar. How much sugar is in 4 cups of the mixture?

Answers can be found on pages 77–78.

Multiple Ratios: Make a Common Term

You may encounter two ratios containing a common element. To combine the ratios, you can use a process remarkably similar to creating a common denominator for fractions.

Because ratios act like fractions, you can multiply both sides of a ratio (or all sides, if there are more than two) by the same number, just as you can multiply the numerator and denominator of a fraction by the same number. You can change *fractions* to have common *denominators*. Likewise, you can change *ratios* to have common *terms* corresponding to the same quantity. Consider the following problem:

> In a box containing action figures of the three Fates from Greek mythology, there are three figures of
> Clotho for every two figures of Atropos, and five figures of Clotho for every four figures of Lachesis.
> (a)   What is the least number of action figures that could be in the box?
> (b)   What is the ratio of Lachesis figures to Atropos figures?

(a) In symbols, this problem tells you that $C : A = 3 : 2$ and $C : L = 5 : 4$. You cannot instantly combine these ratios into a single ratio of all three quantities, because the terms for C are different. However, you can fix that problem by multiplying each ratio by the right number, making both C's into the *least common multiple* of the current values.

$$
\begin{array}{llll}
C : A : L & & & C : A : L \\
3 : 2 & \rightarrow \quad \text{Multiply by 5} \rightarrow & & 15 : 10 \\
5 : \quad : 4 & \rightarrow \quad \text{Multiply by 3} \rightarrow & & 15 : \quad : 12
\end{array}
$$

This is the combined ratio: $\boxed{15 : 10 : 12}$

The actual *numbers* of action figures are these three numbers times an Unknown Multiplier, which must be a positive integer. Using the smallest possible multiplier, 1, there are $15 + 12 + 10 = 37$ action figures.

(b) Once you have combined the ratios, you can extract the numbers corresponding to the quantities in question and disregard the others: $L : A = 12 : 10$, which reduces to $6 : 5$.

Check Your Skills

6. A school has 3 freshmen for every 4 sophomores and 5 sophomores for every 4 juniors. If there are 240 juniors in the school, how many freshmen are there?

Answer can be found on page 78.

Check Your Skills Answers

1. **25:** Set up a proportion:

$$\frac{3\,\text{apples}}{5\,\text{oranges}} = \frac{15\,\text{apples}}{x\,\text{oranges}}$$

Now cross multiply:

$$3x = 5 \times 15$$
$$3x = 75$$
$$x = 25$$

2. **35:** Set up a proportion:

$$\frac{7\,\text{jazz}}{12\,\text{classical}} = \frac{x\,\text{jazz}}{60\,\text{classical}}$$

Now cross multiply:

$$7 \times 60 = 12x$$
$$420 = 12x$$
$$35 = x$$

3. **30:** Using the unknown multiplier, label the number of apples $3x$ and the number of oranges $5x$. Make a quick table:

Apples	+	Oranges	=	Total
$3x$	+	$5x$	=	$8x$

The total is equal to $8x$, and there are 48 total fruit, so

$$8x = 48$$
$$x = 6$$
$$\text{Oranges} = 5x = 5(6) = 30$$

4. **48:** Using the unknown multiplier, label the number of nuts $5x$, the number of bolts $4x$ and the number of washers $6x$. The total is $5x + 4x + 6x$.

$$5x + 4x + 6x = 180$$
$$15x = 180$$
$$x = 12$$

The total number of bolts is $4(12) = 48$

5. **8/5:** Using the unknown multiplier, label the amount of flour $3x$, and the amount of sugar $2x$. The total amount of mixture is $3x + 2x = 5x$.

$5x = 4$ (cups)
$x = 4/5$

The total amount of sugar is $2(4/5) = 8/5$ cups.

6. **225:** Use a table to organize the different ratios:

F : S : J	
3 : 4	(3 freshmen for every 4 sophomores)
5 : 4	(5 sophomores for every 4 juniors)

Sophomores appear in both ratios, as 4 in the first and 5 in the second. The lowest common denominator of 4 and 5 is 20. Multiply the ratios accordingly:

F : S : J			F : S : J
3 : 4	→ Multiply by 5 →		15 : 20
5 : 4	→ Multiply by 4 →		20 : 16

The final ratio is F : S : J = 15 : 20 : 16. There are 240 juniors. Use a ratio to solve for the number of freshmen:

$$\frac{16}{240} = \frac{15}{x}$$

$$\frac{1}{15} = \frac{15}{x}$$

$$x = 225$$

*Manhattan*GRE Prep
the new standard

Problem Set

Solve the following problems, using the strategies you have learned in this section. Use proportions and the unknown multiplier to organize ratios.

For problems 1 through 5, assume that neither x nor y is equal to 0, to permit division by x and by y.

1. 48 : 2x is equivalent to 144 : 600. What is x?

2. x : 15 is equivalent to y to x. Given that $y = 3x$, what is x?

3. Brian's marbles have a red to yellow ratio of 2 : 1. If Brian has 22 red marbles, how many yellow marbles does Brian have?

4. Initially, the men and women in a room were in the ratio of 5 : 7. Six women leave the room. If there are 35 men in the room, how many women are left in the room?

5. It is currently raining cats and dogs in the ratio of 5 : 6. If there are 18 fewer cats than dogs, how many dogs are raining?

6. The amount of time that three people worked on a special project was in the ratio of 2 to 3 to 5. If the project took 110 hours, how many more hours did the hardest working person work than the person who worked the least?

7.

A group of students and teachers take a field trip, such that the student to teacher ratio is 8 to 1. The total number of people on the field trip is between 60 and 70.

Quantity A	**Quantity B**
The number of teachers on the field trip	6

8.

The ratio of men to women on a panel was 3 to 4 before one woman was replaced by a man.

Quantity A	**Quantity B**
The number of men on the panel	The number of women on the panel

9.

A bracelet contains rubies, emeralds
and sapphires, such that there are
two rubies for every emerald and five
sapphires for every three rubies.

Quantity A

The minimum possible number of
gemstones on the bracelet

Quantity B

20

1. **100:**

$$\frac{48}{2x} = \frac{144}{600}$$ Simplify the ratios and cancel factors horizontally across the equals sign.

$$\frac{\cancel{24}\ 4}{x} = \frac{\cancel{6}\ 1}{25}$$ Then, cross-multiply: $x = 100$.

2. **45:**

$$\frac{x}{15} = \frac{y}{x}$$ First, substitute $3x$ for y.

$$\frac{x}{15} = \frac{3x}{x} = 3$$ Then, solve for x: $x = 3 \times 15 = 45$.

3. **11:** Write a proportion to solve this problem: $\dfrac{\text{red}}{\text{yellow}} = \dfrac{2}{1} = \dfrac{22}{x}$

   Cross-multiply to solve: $2x = 22$
   $$x = 11$$

4. **43:** First, establish the starting number of men and women with a proportion, and simplify.

$$\frac{5 \text{ men}}{7 \text{ women}} = \frac{35 \text{ men}}{x \text{ women}} \qquad \frac{\cancel{5}\ 1 \text{ man}}{7 \text{ women}} = \frac{\cancel{35}\ 7 \text{ men}}{x \text{ women}}$$

   Cross-multiply: $x = 49$.

If 6 women leave the room, there are $49 - 6 = 43$ women left.

5. **108:** If the ratio of cats to dogs is 5 : 6, then there are $5x$ cats and $6x$ dogs (using the Unknown Multiplier). Express the fact that there are 18 fewer cats than dogs with an equation:

$$5x + 18 = 6x$$
$$x = 18$$

Therefore, there are $6(18) = 108$ dogs.

6. **33 hours:** Use an equation with the Unknown Multiplier to represent the total hours put in by the three people:

$$2x + 3x + 5x = 110$$
$$10x = 110$$
$$x = 11$$

Therefore, the hardest working person put in 5(11) = 55 hours, and the person who worked the least put in 2(11) = 22 hours. This represents a difference of 55 − 22 = 33 hours.

7. **A:** We can use an Unknown Multiplier x to help express the number of students and teachers. In light of the given ratio there would be x teachers and $8x$ students, and the total number of people on the field trip would therefore be $x + 8x = 9x$. Note that x in this case must be a positive integer, because we cannot have fractional people.

The total number of people must therefore be a multiple of 9. The only multiple of 9 between 60 and 70 is 63. Therefore x must be 63/9 = 7. Rewrite the columns:

Quantity A	Quantity B
The number of teachers on the field trip = 7	6

Therefore, **Quantity A is larger.**

8. **D:** While we know the ratio of men to women, we do not know the actual number of men and women. The following Before and After charts illustrate two of many possibilities:

Case 1	Men	Women
Before	3	4
After	4	3

Case 2	Men	Women
Before	9	12
After	10	11

These charts illustrate that the number of men may or may not be greater than the number of women after the move. **We do not have enough information** to answer the question.

9. **B:** This Multiple Ratio problem is complicated by the fact that the number of rubies is not consistent between the two given ratios, appearing as 2 in one and 3 in the other. We can use the least common multiple of 2 and 3 to make the number of rubies the same in both ratios:

$E : R : S$ $E : R : S$
1 : 2   multiply by 3   3 : 6
   3 : 5   multiply by 2   6 : 10

Combining the two ratios into a single ratio yields:

$E : R : S :$ Total = 3 : 6 : 10 : 19

The smallest possible total number of gemstones is 19. Therefore **Quantity B is greater.**

g | **Chapter 5**
of
WORD PROBLEMS

STATISTICS

In This Chapter . . .

Averages

The **average** (or the **arithmetic mean**) of a set is given by the following formula (also known as "the average formula"):

$$\text{Average} = \frac{\text{Sum}}{\text{\# of terms}}, \text{ which is abbreviated as } A = \frac{S}{n}.$$

The sum, S, refers to the sum of all the terms in the set.
The number, n, refers to the number of terms that are in the set.
The average, A, refers to the average value (arithmetic mean) of the terms in the set.

The language in an average problem will often refer to an "arithmetic mean." However, occasionally the concept is implied. "The cost per employee, if equally shared, is $20" means that the <u>average</u> cost per employee is $20.

A commonly used variation of the Average formula is:

$$(\text{Average}) \times (\text{\# of terms}) = (\text{Sum}), \text{ or } A \cdot n = S.$$

This formula has the same basic form as the $RT = D$ equation, so it lends itself readily to the same kind of table you would use for RTD problems.

Every GRE problem dealing with averages can be solved with the average formula. If you are asked to use or find the average of a set, you should not generally concentrate on the individual terms of the set. As you can see from the formulas above, all that matters is the *sum* of the terms—which can often be found even if the individual terms cannot be determined.

Using the Average Formula

The first thing to do for any GRE average problem is to write down the average formula. Then, fill in any of the 3 variables (S, n, and A) that are given in the problem.

> The sum of 6 numbers is 90. What is the average term?

$$A = \frac{S}{n}$$

The sum, S, is given as 90. The number of terms, n, is given as 6.

By plugging in, we can solve for the average: $\frac{90}{6} = 15$.

Notice that you do NOT need to know each term in the set to find the average!

Sometimes, using the average formula will be more involved. For example:

> If the average of the set {2, 5, 5, 7, 8, 9, x} is 6.1, what is the value of x?

Plug the given information into the average formula, and solve for x.

$$(6.1)(7 \text{ terms}) = 2 + 5 + 5 + 7 + 8 + 9 + x$$

$$A \cdot n = S \qquad\qquad 42.7 = 36 + x$$

$$6.7 = x$$

More complex average problems involve setting up two average formulas. For example:

> Sam earned a $2,000 commission on a big sale, raising his average commission by $100. If Sam's new average commission is $900, how many sales has he made?

To keep track of two average formulas in the same problem, you can set up an *RTD*-style table. Instead of *RT* = *D*, we use $A \cdot n = S$, which has the same form.

Note that the Number and Sum columns add up to give the new cumulative values, but the values in the Average column do *not* add up:

	Average	×	Number	=	Sum
Old Total	800	×	n	=	800n
This Sale	2000	×	1	=	2000
New Total	900	×	$n + 1$	=	900($n + 1$)

The right-hand column gives the equation we need:

$$800n + 2000 = 900(n + 1)$$
$$800n + 2000 = 900n + 900$$
$$1100 = 100n$$
$$11 = n$$

Since we are looking for the new number of sales, which is $n + 1$, Sam has made a total of 12 sales.

Check Your Skills

1. The sum of 6 integers is 45. What is the average of the six integers?
2. The average price per item in a shopping basket is $2.40. If there are a total of 30 items in the basket, what is the total price of the items in the basket?

Answers can be found on page 93.

Evenly Spaced Sets: Take the Middle

You may recall that the average of a set of consecutive integers is the middle number (the middle number of <u>any</u> set is always its median – more on this later). This is true for any set in which the terms are spaced evenly apart. For example:

The average of the set {3, 5, 7, 9, 11} is the middle term 7, because all the terms in the set are spaced evenly apart (in this case, they are spaced 2 units apart).

The average of the set {12, 20, 28, 36, 44, 52, 60, 68, 76} is the middle term 44, because all the terms in the set are spaced evenly apart (in this case, they are spaced 8 units apart).

Note that if an evenly spaced set has two "middle" numbers, the average of the set is the average of these two middle numbers. For example:

The average of the set {5, 10, 15, 20, 25, 30} is 17.5, because this is the average of the two middle numbers: 15 and 20.

You do not have to write out each term of an evenly spaced set to find the middle number—the average term. All you need to do to find the middle number is to add the **first** and **last** terms and divide that sum by 2. For example:

The average of the set {101, 111, 121...581, 591, 601} is equal to 351, which is the sum of the first and last terms (101 + 601 = 702) divided by 2. This approach is especially attractive if the number of terms is large.

Check Your Skills

3. What is the average of the set {2, 5, 8, 11, 14}?
4. What is the average of the set {−1, 3, 7, 11, 15, 19, 23, 27}?

Answers can be found on page 93.

Weighted Averages

PROPERTIES OF WEIGHTED AVERAGES

Although weighted averages differ from traditional averages, they are still averages—meaning that their values will still fall *between* the values being averaged (or between the highest and lowest of those values, if there are more than two).

A weighted average of only *two* values will fall closer to whichever value is weighted more heavily. For instance, if a drink is made by mixing 2 shots of a liquor containing 15% alcohol with 3 shots of a liquor containing 20% alcohol, then the alcohol content of the mixed drink will be closer to 20% than to 15%.

Here's another example, take the weighted average of 20 and 30, with weights $\dfrac{a}{a+b}$ and $\dfrac{b}{a+b}$.

$$\text{Weighted average} = \frac{a}{a+b}(20) + \frac{b}{a+b}(30)$$

The weighted average will always be between 20 and 30, as long as a and b are both positive (and on the GRE, they always have been). A number line between 20 and 30 displays where the weighted average will fall:

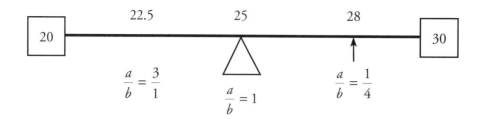

Check Your Skills

5. A stock portfolio is comprised of Stock A, whose annual gain was 10%, and Stock B, whose annual gain was 20%. If the stock portfolio gained 14% overall, does it contain more shares of Stock A or Stock B?
6. 2/3 of the aliens on Planet X are Zorgs, whose average IQ is 120. The rest are Weebs, whose average IQ is 180. What is the average IQ of all the aliens on Planet X?

Answers can be found on page 93.

Median: The Middle Number

Some GRE problems feature a second type of average: the *median*, or "middle value." The median is calculated in one of two ways, depending on the number of data points in the set.

For sets containing an **odd** number of values, the median is the **unique middle value** when the data are arranged in increasing (or decreasing) order.

For sets containing an **even** number of values, the median is the **average (arithmetic mean) of the two middle values** when the data are arranged in increasing (or decreasing) order.

The median of the set {5, 17, 24, 25, 28} is the unique middle number, 24. The median of the set {3, 4, 9, 9} is the mean of the two middle values (4 and 9), or 6.5. Notice that the median of a set containing an *odd* number of values must be a value in the set. However, the median of a set containing an *even* number of values does not have to be in the set—and indeed *will not be*, unless the two middle values are equal.

Medians of Sets Containing Unknown Values

Unlike the arithmetic mean, the median of a set depends only on the one or two values in the middle of the ordered set. Therefore, you may be able to determine a specific value for the median of a set *even if one or more unknowns are present*.

For instance, consider the unordered set {x, 2, 5, 11, 11, 12, 33}. No matter whether x is less than 11, equal to 11, or greater than 11, the median of the resulting set will be 11. (Try substituting different values of x to see why the median does not change.)

By contrast, the median of the unordered set {x, 2, 5, 11, 12, 12, 33} depends on x. If x is 11 or less, the median is 11. If x is between 11 and 12, the median is x. Finally, if x is 12 or more, the median is 12.

Check Your Skills

7. What is the median of the set {6, 2, −1, 4, 0}?
8. What is the median of the set {1, 2, x, 8}, if $2 < x < 8$?

Answers can be found on page 93.

Standard Deviation

The mean and median both give "average" or "representative" values for a set, but they do not tell the whole story. It is possible for two sets to have the same average but to differ widely in how spread out their values are. To describe the spread, or variation, of the data in a set, we use a different measure: the Standard Deviation.

Standard Deviation (SD) indicates how far from the average (mean) the data points typically fall. Therefore:

A small SD indicates that a set is clustered closely around the average (mean) value.

A large SD indicates that the set is spread out widely, with some points appearing far from the mean.

Consider the sets {5, 5, 5, 5}, {2, 4, 6, 8}, and {0, 0, 10, 10}. These sets all have the same mean value of 5. You can see at a glance, though, that the sets are very different, and the differences are reflected in their SDs. The first set has a SD of zero (no spread at all), the second set has a moderate SD, and the third set has a large SD.

The formula for calculating SD is rather cumbersome. The good news is that you do not need to know—**it is very unlikely that a GRE problem will ask you to calculate an exact SD**. If you just pay attention to what the *average spread* is doing, you should be able to answer all GRE standard deviation problems, which involve either (a) *changes* in the SD when a set is transformed or (b) *comparisons* of the SDs of two or more sets. Just remember that the more spread out the numbers, the larger the SD.

If you see a problem focusing on changes in the SD, ask yourself whether the changes move the data closer to the mean, farther from the mean, or neither. If you see a problem requiring comparisons, ask yourself which set is more spread out from its mean.

You should also know the term "variance," which is just the <u>square</u> of the standard deviation.

Following are some sample problems to help illustrate standard deviation properties:

(a) Which set has the greater standard deviation: {1, 2, 3, 4, 5} or {440, 442, 443, 444, 445}?
(b) If each data point in a set is increased by 7, does the set's standard deviation increase, decrease, or remain constant?
(c) If each data point in a set is increased by a factor of 7, does the set's standard deviation increase, decrease, or remain constant?

(a) The second set has the greater SD. One way to understand this is to observe that the gaps between its numbers are, on average, slightly bigger than the gaps in the first set (because the first 2 numbers are 2 units apart). Another way to resolve the issue is to observe that the set {441, 442, 443, 444, 445} would have the same standard deviation as {1, 2, 3, 4, 5}. Replacing 441 with 440, which is farther from the mean, will increase the SD.

In any case, only the *spread* matters. The numbers in the second set are much more "consistent" in some sense—they are all within about 1% of each other, while the largest numbers in the first set are several times the smallest ones. However, this "percent variation" idea is irrelevant to the SD.

(b) The SD will not change. "Increased by 7" means that the number 7 is *added* to each data point in the set. This transformation will not affect any of the gaps between the data points, and thus it will not affect how far the data points are from the mean. If the set were plotted on a number line, this transformation would merely slide the points 7 units to the right, taking all the gaps, and the mean, along with them.

(c) The SD will increase. "Increased by a *factor* of 7" means that each data point is multiplied by 7. This transformation will make all the gaps between points 7 times as big as they originally were. Thus, each point will fall 7 times as far from the mean. The SD will increase by a factor of 7.

Check Your Skills

9. Which set has a greater standard deviation?
>   Set A: {3, 4, 5, 6, 7}   Set B: {3, 3, 5, 7, 7}
>   *Answers can be found on page 94.*

Range

The range of a set of numbers is another measure of the dispersion of the set of numbers. It is defined simply as the difference between the largest number in the set and the smallest number in the set. For example, in the set {3 ,6, −1, 4, 12, 8}, the largest number is 12 and the smallest number is −1. Therefore the range is $12 − (−1) = 13$.

Check Your Skills

10. The set {2, −1, *x*, 5, 3} has a range of 13. What are the possible values for *x*?
>   *Answers can be found on page 94.*

Quartiles and Percentiles

Sets of numbers can be described by Quartiles and, for larger sets, by Percentiles. For example, consider the following set of 16 numbers:

$$\left\{ \underbrace{0, 1, 2, 2}_{\text{Quartile 1}} \mid \underbrace{3, 4, 5, 5}_{\text{Quartile 2}} \mid \underbrace{5, 6, 7, 8}_{\text{Quartile 3}} \mid \underbrace{10, 11, 13, 14}_{\text{Quartile 4}} \right\}$$

$$Q_1 \qquad\qquad Q_2 \qquad\qquad Q_3$$

As you can see the set is divided into four quartiles, each divided with "Quartile Markers." Q_1 is the average of the highest item in Quartile 1 and the lowest item in Quartile 2, and so on. Thus $Q_1 = \dfrac{2+3}{2} = 2.5$, $Q_2 = \dfrac{5+5}{2} = 5$, and $Q_3 = \dfrac{8+10}{2} = 9$. As you can see, Q_2 is *the same as* the median of the set.

For larger sets (of, say, 1,000 numbers), Percentiles can be used. Thus in a set of 1,000 numbers, the 10 smallest items will be in Percentile 1, and P_1 will be the average of the 10th and 11th smallest items. Note that $P_{25} = Q_1$, $P_{50} = Q_2 = $ median, and $P_{75} = Q_3$.

Check Your Skills

11. In the set {2, 3, 0, 8, 11, 1, 4, 7, 8, 2, 1, 3}, what is $Q_3 − Q_1$?
>   *Answers can be found on page 94.*

The Normal Distribution

One of the most important distributions for random variables is the Normal Distribution (also known as the Gaussian Distribution). The Normal Distribution looks like the classic "bell-curve," rounded in the middle with long tails, and symmetric around the mean (which equals the median).

Normal Distribution with Mean = 10 and Standard Deviation = 4

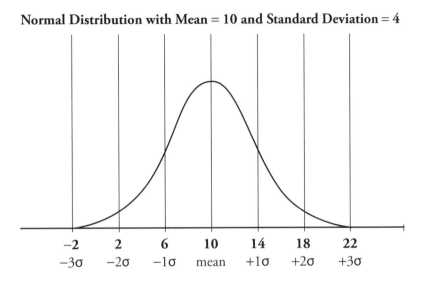

The GRE tests on distributions that are both <u>normal</u> and <u>approximately normal</u>. These distributions have the following characteristics:

- The <u>mean</u> and <u>median</u> are **equal**, or *almost exactly* equal.

- The data is exactly, or *almost exactly*, symmetric around the mean/median.

- Roughly $\frac{2}{3}$ of the sample will fall within 1 standard deviation of the mean. Thus in the above example, a value of 6 is at roughly $50\% - \left(\frac{1}{2}\right)\left(\frac{2}{3}\right) \approx 17\%$, or the 17th Percentile. A value of 14 is at roughly $50\% + \left(\frac{1}{2}\right)\left(\frac{2}{3}\right) \approx 83\%$, or the 83rd Percentile.

- Roughly 96% of the sample will fall within 2 standard deviations of the mean. Thus a value of 2 will be at the $50\% - \left(\frac{1}{2}\right)(96\%) = 2\%$ or 2nd Percentile, and a value of 18 will be at the $50 + \left(\frac{1}{2}\right)(96\%) = 98\%$, or 98th Percentile.

- Only about $\frac{1}{1,000}$ (0.1%) of the curve is 3 or more standard deviations below the mean; the same is true above the mean.

The GRE will only generally test these concepts in a general way, and will not distinguish between random variables that are normally distributed versus ones that are <u>nearly</u> normally distributed. However, it is <u>important</u> to note that distributions that are <u>not</u> normal or nearly normal do <u>not</u> necessarily share the above characteristics. It is possible, for example to construct distributions where the mean and median are substantially different, or where 100% of the observations fall within 2 standard deviations, or where more than 1% of the observations fall more than 3 standard deviations from the mean.

Check Your Skills

12. Variable X is nearly normally distributed, with a mean of 6 and a standard deviation of 2. Approximately what percent of the observation in X will be smaller than 4?

13. Approximately what percent will be greater than 12?

14. Approximately what percentile corresponds to a value of 2?

15. Would the answers to questions 12–14, above, be the same if Variable X were <u>not</u> nearly normally distributed?

Answers can be found on page 94.

Check Your Skills Answers

1. **7.5:** $A = \dfrac{S}{n}$

$$A = \frac{45}{6} = 7.5$$

2. **$72:** $A = \dfrac{S}{n}$

$$2.40 = \frac{S}{30}$$
$$S = 2.40(30) = 72$$

3. **8:** Notice that each term in the set is 3 more than the last. Because this set is evenly spaced, the median and the average will be the same. The median is 8, and so the average is also 8.

4. **13:** Notice that each term in the set is 4 more than the last. Because this set is evenly spaced, the median and the average will be the same. The number of terms in the set is even, so the median of the set is the average of the two middle terms: $A = (11 + 15)/2 = 13$.

5. **Stock A:** Because the overall gain is closer to 10% than to 20%, the portfolio must be weighted more heavily towards Stock A, i.e., contain more shares of Stock A.

6. **140:** 2/3 of the total population is Zorgs, and so the weight is 2/3. Similarly, the weight of the Weebs is 1/3. Now plug everything into the weighted average formula:

$$\text{Weighted Average} = \frac{2}{3}(120) + \frac{1}{3}(120)$$
$$= 80 + 60$$
$$= 140$$

7. **2:** First order the set from least to greatest:

$$\{6, 2, -1, 4, 0\} \rightarrow \{-1, 0, 2, 4, 6\}$$

The median is the middle number, which is 2.

8. $\dfrac{2+x}{2}$ **or** $1+\dfrac{x}{2}$**:** Because the number of terms is even, the median is the average of the two middle terms:

$\dfrac{2+4}{2} = 3$. Since $2 < x < 8$, the lower of the two middle terms will be 2 and the higher of the two middle terms will

be x. Therefore the median is $\dfrac{2+x}{2}$, or $1+\dfrac{x}{2}$.

9. **Set B:** Each set has a mean of 5, so the set whose numbers are further away from the mean will have the higher standard deviation. When comparing standard deviations, focus on the differences between each set. The numbers that each set has in common are highlighted:

       Set A: {**3**, 4, **5**, 6, **7**}   Set B: {**3**, 3, **5**, 7, **7**}

Compare the numbers that are not the same. 4 and 6 in Set A are closer to the mean (5) than are 3 and 7 in Set B. Therefore, the numbers in Set B are further away from the mean and Set B has a larger standard deviation.

10. **12 or −8:** If x is the smallest number, then 5 is the largest number in the set and $5 - x = 13$, so $x = -8$. If x is the largest number, then −1 is the smallest number in the set and $x - (-1) = 13$, so $x = 12$.

11. **6:** The first thing to do is to list the set elements in order, then determine the cutoff points for Q_1, Q_2, and Q_3.

$$\{0, 1, 1,|2, 2, 3,|3, 4, 7,|8, 8, 11\}$$
$$\quad\quad\quad Q_1 \quad\quad Q_2 \quad\quad Q_3$$

$$Q_3 = \frac{7+8}{2} = 7.5$$

$$Q_1 = \frac{1+2}{2} = 1.5$$

Therefore $Q_3 - Q_1 = 6$.

12. **17%:** $50\% - \left(\frac{1}{2}\right)\left(\frac{2}{3}\right) = 17\%$.

13. **Approximately 0.1%:** Roughly, 1 in 1,000 observations in a normal distribution will be 3 standard deviations above the mean.

14. **2nd Percentile:** Approximately $50\% - \left(\frac{1}{2}\right)(96\%) = 2\%$, or 2nd Percentile.

15. **No, not necessarily.**

Problem Set

1.   The average of 11 numbers is 10. When one number is eliminated, the average of the remaining numbers is 9.3. What is the eliminated number?

2.   The average of 9, 11, and 16 is equal to the average of 21, 4.6, and what number?

3.   Given the set of numbers {4, 5, 5, 6, 7, 8, 21}, how much higher is the mean than the median?

4.   The sum of 8 numbers is 168. If one of the numbers is 28, what is the average of the other 7 numbers?

5.   If the average of the set {5, 6, 6, 8, 9, x, y} is 6, then what is the value of $x + y$?

6.   On 4 sales, Matt received commissions of $300, $40, $$x$, and $140. Without the $$x$, his average commission would be $50 lower. What is x?

7.   The class mean score on a test was 60, and the standard deviation was 15. If Elena's score was within 2 standard deviations of the mean, what is the lowest score she could have received?

8.   Matt gets a $1,000 commission on a big sale. This commission alone raises his average commission by $150. If Matt's new average commission is $400, how many sales has Matt made?

9.   Grace's average bowling score over the past 6 games is 150. If she wants to raise her average score by 10%, and she has two games left in the season, what must her average score on the last two games be?

10.   If the average of x and y is 50, and the average of y and z is 80, what is the value of $z - x$?

11.   If $x > 0$ and the range of 1, 2, x, 5, and x^2 equals 7, what is the approximate average (mean) of the set?

12.   Among the set {1, 2, 3, 4, 7, 7, 10, 10, 11, 14, 19, 19, 23, 24, 25, 26}, what is the ratio of the largest item in the 2nd Quartile to the average value in the 4th Quartile?

13. N is a normally distributed variable with a mean of 0. If approximately 2% of the observations in N are −10 or smaller, what fraction of the observations are between 0 and 5?

14.

A college class is attended by Poets and Bards in the ratio of three Poets for every two Bards. On a midterm the average score of the Poets is 60 and the average score of the Bards is 80.

Quantity A	**Quantity B**
The overall average score for the class	70

15.

$$x > 2$$

Quantity A	**Quantity B**
The median of $x - 4$, $x + 1$, and $4x$	The mean of $x - 4$, $x + 1$, and $4x$

16.

A is the set of the first five positive odd integers. B is the set of the first five positive even integers.

Quantity A	**Quantity B**
The standard deviation of A	The standard deviation of B

1. **17:** If the average of 11 numbers is 10, their sum is $11 \times 10 = 110$. After one number is eliminated, the average is 9.3, so the sum of the 10 remaining numbers is $10 \times 9.3 = 93$. The number eliminated is the difference between these sums: $110 - 93 = 17$.

2. **10.4:** $\dfrac{9+11+16}{3} = \dfrac{21+4.6+x}{3}$ $9 + 11 + 16 = 21 + 4.6 + x$ $x = 10.4$

3. **2:** The mean of the set is the sum of the numbers divided by the number of terms: $56 \div 7 = 8$. The median is the middle number: 6. 8 is 2 greater than 6.

4. **20:** The sum of the other 7 numbers is 140 ($168 - 28$). So, the average of the numbers is $140/7 = 20$.

5. **8:** If the average of 7 terms is 6, then the sum of the terms is 7×6, or 42. The listed terms have a sum of 34. Therefore, the remaining terms, x and y, must have a sum of $42 - 34$, or 8.

6. **$360:** Without x, Matt's average sale is $(300 + 40 + 140) \div 3$, or $160. With x, Matt's average is $50 more, or $210. Therefore, the sum of $(300 + 40 + 140 + x) = 4(210) = 840$, and $x = \$360$.

7. **30:** Elena's score was within 2 standard deviations of the mean. Since the standard deviation is 15, her score is no more than 30 points from the mean. The lowest possible score she could have received, then, is $60 - 30$, or 30.

8. **5:** Before the $1,000 commission, Matt's average commission was $250; we can express this algebraically with the equation $S = 250n$.

After the sale, the sum of Matt's sales increased by $1,000, the number of sales made increased by 1, and his average commission was $400. We can express this algebraically with the equation:

$$S + 1{,}000 = 400(n + 1)$$

$$250n + 1{,}000 = 400(n + 1)$$
$$250n + 1{,}000 = 400n + 400$$
$$150n = 600$$
$$n = 4$$

Before the big sale, Matt had made 4 sales. Including the big sale, Matt has made 5 sales.

9. **210:** Grace wants to raise her average score by 10%. Since 10% of 150 is 15, her target average is 165. Grace's total score is 150×6, or 900. If, in 8 games, she wants to have an average score of 165, then she will need a total score of 165×8, or 1,320. This is a difference of $1{,}320 - 900$, or 420. Her average score in the next two games must be: $420 \div 2 = 210$.

10. **60:** The sum of two numbers is twice their average. Therefore,

$$x + y = 100 \qquad\qquad y + z = 160$$
$$x = 100 - y \qquad\qquad z = 160 - y$$

Substitute these expressions for z and x:

$$z - x = (160 - y) - (100 - y) = 160 - y - 100 + y = 160 - 100 = 60$$

Alternatively, pick Smart Numbers for x and y. Let $x = 50$ and $y = 50$ (this is an easy way to make their average equal 50). Since the average of y and z must be 80, we have $z = 110$. Therefore, $z - x = 110 - 50 = 60$.

11. **3.76:** If the range of the set is 7 and $x > 0$, then x^2 has to be the largest number in the set and $x^2 - 1 = 7$.

Therefore $x^2 = 8$, and $x = 2\sqrt{2}$. The average of the set is thus $\dfrac{1 + 2 + 2\sqrt{2} + 5 + 8}{5} = \dfrac{16 + 2\sqrt{2}}{5}$, which is approximately $3.2 + \dfrac{2.8}{5}$, or 3.76.

12. $\dfrac{20}{49}$: Since the set is given in order, we can see that the largest item in the 2nd Quartile is the eighth item in the

list, which is 10. Furthermore the items in the 4th Quartile are 23, 24, 25, and 26, and their average is

$\dfrac{23 + 24 + 25 + 26}{4} = 24.5$. (Note that these numbers are an evenly spaced set, so the average equals the median or

middle number.)

The ratio is thus $\dfrac{10}{24.5} = \dfrac{20}{49}$.

13. $\dfrac{1}{3}$: If 2% of the observations are below -10, then -10 must approximately be 2 standard deviations from the

mean. Thus the standard deviation is approximately $\dfrac{|-10|}{2} \approx 5$, and thus roughly $\dfrac{2}{3}$ of the observations will fall

between -5 and 5. Since normal variables are symmetric around the mean, half of that will be in the 0–5 range, so

the correct answer is $\left(\dfrac{1}{2}\right)\left(\dfrac{2}{3}\right) = \dfrac{1}{3}$.

14. **B:** This is a Weighted Average problem. The overall average score can be computed by assigning weights to the average scores of Poets and Bards that reflect the number of people in each subgroup. Because the ratio of Poets to Bards is 3 to 2, and collectively the two groups account for all students, the multiple ratio may be written as $P : B : Total = 3 : 2 : 5$.

This means that Poets constitute 3/5 of the students and Bards the remaining 2/5. Therefore, the overall average score is given by the weighted average formula:

$$\frac{3}{5} \times 60 + \frac{2}{5} \times 80 = 68$$

Alternatively, we may argue as follows: if there were the same number of Poets as there were Bards, the overall average score would be 70. However, there are actually more Poets than Bards, so the overall average score will be closer to 60 than to 80, i.e., less than 70. Therefore **Quantity B is greater.**

15. **B:** Let us begin with the median. In a set with an odd number of terms, the median will be the middle term when the terms are put in ascending order. It is clear that $x + 1 > x - 4$. Moreover, because $x > 2$, $4x$ must be greater than $x + 1$. Therefore the median is $x + 1$. Rewrite Quantity A:

Quantity A	**Quantity B**
The median of $x - 4$, $x + 1$, and $4x = x + 1$	The mean of $x - 4$, $x + 1$, and $4x$

In order to compute the mean, we add all three terms and divide by 3:

$$\text{Mean} = \frac{(x-4)+(x+1)+4x}{3} = \frac{6x-3}{3} = 2x - 1$$

Rewrite Quantity B:

Quantity A	**Quantity B**
The median of $x - 4$, $x + 1$, and $4x = \boldsymbol{x + 1}$	The mean of $x - 4$, $x + 1$, and $4x = \boldsymbol{2x - 1}$

The comparison thus boils down to which is larger, $x + 1$ or $2x - 1$. The answer is not immediately clear. Subtract x from both sides to try and isolate x.

Quantity A	**Quantity B**
$x + 1$	$2x - 1$
$\underline{-x}$	$\underline{-x}$
1	$x - 1$

Now add one to both sides to isolate x:

Quantity A	**Quantity B**
$1 + 1 = \boldsymbol{2}$	$(x - 1) + 1 = \boldsymbol{x}$

The question stem states that x must be larger than 2, so **Quantity B must be larger**.

16. **C:** The sets in question are $A = \{1, 3, 5, 7, 9\}$ and $B = \{2, 4, 6, 8, 10\}$. Each is a set of evenly spaced integers with an odd number of terms, such that the mean is the middle number. The deviations between the elements of the set and the mean of the set in each case are the same: -4, -2, 0, 2 and 4. Thus the standard deviations of the sets must also be the same. The **two quantities are equal.**

Chapter 6
of
WORD PROBLEMS

COMBINATORICS

In This Chapter . . .

- The Fundamental Counting Principle
- Simple Factorials
- Anagrams
- Combinatorics with Repetition: Anagram Grids
- Multiple Arrangements

COMBINATORICS

Many GRE problems are, ultimately, just about counting things. Although counting may seem to be a simple concept, *problems about counting* can be complex. In fact, counting problems have given rise to a whole sub-field of mathematics: *combinatorics*, which is essentially "advanced counting." This chapter presents the fundamentals of combinatorics that are essential on the GRE.

In combinatorics, we are often counting the **number of possibilities**, such as: How many different ways you can arrange things? For instance, we might ask the following:

(1)   A restaurant menu features five appetizers, six entrées, and three desserts. If a dinner special consists of one appetizer, one entrée, and one dessert, how many different dinner specials are possible?

(2)   Four people sit down in 4 fixed chairs lined up in a row. How many different seating arrangements are possible?

(3)   If there are 7 people in a room, but only 3 chairs in a row, how many different seating arrangements are possible?

(4)   If a group of 3 people is to be chosen from 7 people in a room, how many different groups are possible?

The Fundamental Counting Principle

Counting problems commonly feature multiple separate choices. Whether such choices are made simultaneously (e.g., choosing types of bread and filling for a sandwich) or sequentially (e.g., choosing among routes between successive towns on a road trip), the rule for counting the number of options is the same.

Fundamental Counting Principle: If you must make a number of *separate* decisions, then MULTIPLY the numbers of ways to make each *individual* decision to find the number of ways to make *all* the decisions.

To grasp this principle intuitively, imagine that you are making a simple sandwich. You will choose ONE type of bread out of 2 types (Rye or Whole wheat) and ONE type of filling out of 3 types (Chicken salad, Peanut butter, or Tuna fish). How many different kinds of sandwich can you make? Well, you can always list all the possibilities:

Rye – Chicken salad   Whole wheat – Chicken salad
Rye – Peanut butter   Whole wheat – Peanut butter
Rye – Tuna fish   Whole wheat – Tuna fish

We see that there are 6 possible sandwiches overall in this table. Instead of listing all the sandwiches, you can simply **multiply** the number of bread choices by the number of filling choices, as dictated by the Fundamental Counting Principle:

2 breads × 3 fillings = 6 possible sandwiches.

As its name implies, the Fundamental Counting Principle is essential to solving combinatorics problems. It is the basis of many other techniques that appear later in this chapter. You can also use the Fundamental Counting Principle directly.

A restaurant menu features five appetizers, six entrées, and three desserts. If a dinner special consists of one appetizer, one entrée, and one dessert, how many different dinner specials are possible?

This problem features three decisions: an appetizer (which can be chosen in 5 different ways), an entrée (6 ways), and a dessert (3 ways). Since the choices are separate, the total number of dinner specials is the product 5 × 6 × 3 = 90.

In theory, you could *list* all 90 dinner specials. In practice, that is the last thing you would ever want to do! It would take far too long, and it is likely that you would make a mistake. Multiplying is *much* easier—and more accurate.

Check Your Skills

1. How many ways are there of getting from Alphaville to Gammerburg via Betancourt, if there are three roads between Alphaville and Betancourt and four roads between Betancourt and Gammerburg?
2. John can choose between blue, black and brown pants, white, yellow or pink shirts, and whether or not he wears a tie to go with his shirt. How many days can John go without wearing the same combination twice?

Answers can be found on page 107.

Simple Factorials

You are often asked to count the possible arrangements of a set of distinct objects (e.g., "Four people sit down in 4 fixed chairs lined up in a row. How many different seating arrangements are possible?") To count these arrangements, use *factorials*:

The number of ways of putting n distinct objects in order, if there are no restrictions, is $n!$ (n factorial).

The term "n factorial" ($n!$) refers to the product of all the positive integers from 1 through n, inclusive: $n! = (n)(n - 1)(n - 2)...(3)(2)(1)$. You should *memorize* the factorials through 6!:

$$1! = 1 \qquad\qquad 4! = 4 \times 3 \times 2 \times 1 = 24$$
$$2! = 2 \times 1 = 2 \qquad\qquad 5! = 5 \times 4 \times 3 \times 2 \times 1 = 120$$
$$3! = 3 \times 2 \times 1 = 6 \qquad\qquad 6! = 6 \times 5 \times 4 \times 3 \times 2 \times 1 = 720$$

$n!$ counts the rearrangements of n distinct objects as a special (but very common) application of the Slot Method. For example consider the case of $n = 4$, with 4 people and 4 fixed chairs. Let each slot represent a chair. Place any one of the 4 people in the first chair. You now have only 3 choices for the person in the second chair. Next, you have 2 choices for the third chair. Finally, you must put the last person in the last chair: you only have 1 choice. Now multiply together all those separate choices.

Arrangements of 4 people in 4 fixed chairs: $\underline{4} \times \underline{3} \times \underline{2} \times \underline{1} = 4! = 24$

Incidentally, you can certainly use the Slot Method the first few times to ensure that you grasp this formula, but then you should graduate to using the formula directly.

> In staging a house, a real-estate agent must place six different books on a bookshelf. In how many different orders can she arrange the books?

Using the Fundamental Counting Principle, we see that we have 6 choices for the book that goes first, 5 choices for the book that goes next, and so forth. Ultimately, we have this total:

$$6! = \underline{6} \times \underline{5} \times \underline{4} \times \underline{3} \times \underline{2} \times \underline{1} = 720 \text{ different orders.}$$

Check Your Skills

3. In how many different ways can the five Olympic rings be colored Black, Red, Green, Yellow and Blue, without changing the arrangement of the rings themselves?

Answer can be found on page 107.

Anagrams

An *anagram* is a rearrangement of the letters in a word or phrase. (Puzzle enthusiasts require the rearrangement itself to be a meaningful word or phrase, but we are also going to include rearrangements that are total nonsense.) For instance, the word DEDUCTIONS is an anagram of DISCOUNTED, and so is the gibberish "word" CDDEINOSTU.

Now that you know about factorials, you can easily count the anagrams of a simple word with *n* distinct letters: simply compute *n*! (*n* factorial).

> How many different anagrams (meaningful or nonsense) are possible for the word GRE?

Since there are 3 distinct letters in the word GRE, there are 3! = 6 anagrams of the word.

Check Your Skills

4. In how many different ways can the letters of the word DEPOSIT be arranged (meaningful or nonsense)?
Answer can be found on page 107.

Combinatorics with Repetition: Anagram Grids

Anagrams themselves are unlikely to appear on the GRE. However, many combinatorics problems are exact analogues of anagram problems and can therefore be solved with the same methods developed for the preceding problem. *Most problems involving rearranging objects can be solved by anagramming.*

> If seven people board an airport shuttle with only three available seats, how many different seating arrangements are possible? (Assume that three of the seven will actually take the seats.)

Three of the people will take the seats (designated 1, 2, and 3), and the other four will be left standing (designated "S"). The problem is therefore equivalent to finding anagrams of the "word" *123SSSS*, where the four S's are equivalent and indistinguishable. *Therefore, we have to "uncount" different arrangements of them when calculating the number of possible arrangements*. You can construct an **Anagram Grid** to help you make the connection:

Person	A	B	C	D	E	F	G
Seat	1	2	3	S	S	S	S

The top row corresponds to the 7 unique people. The bottom row corresponds to the "seating labels" that we put on those people. Note that some of these labels are repeated (the four S's). In general, you should set up an Anagram Grid to put the unique items or people on top. Only the bottom row should contain any repeated labels.

In this grid, you are free to rearrange the elements in the bottom row (the three seat numbers and the four S's), making "anagrams" that represent all the possible seating arrangements. The number of arrangements is therefore:

$$\frac{7!}{4!} = \frac{7 \times 6 \times 5 \times 4 \times 3 \times 2 \times 1}{4 \times 3 \times 2 \times 1} = 7 \times 6 \times 5 = 210$$

Again, we divide by 4! Because the 4! ways of arranging the S's are <u>irrelevant.</u>

Now consider this problem:

> If three of seven standby passengers are selected for a flight, how many different combinations of standby passengers can be selected?

At first, this problem may seem identical to the previous one, because it also involves selecting 3 elements out of a set of 7. However, there is a crucial difference. This time, the three "chosen ones" are *also* indistinguishable, whereas in the earlier problem, the three seats on the shuttle were considered different. As a result, you designate all three flying passengers as *F*'s. The four non-flying passengers are still designated as *N*'s. The problem is then equivalent to finding anagrams of the "word" *FFFNNNN*. Again, you can use an Anagram Grid:

Person	A	B	C	D	E	F	G
Seat	F	F	F	N	N	N	N

To calculate the number of possibilities, we follow the same rule—factorial of the total, divided by the factorials of the repeated letters on the bottom. But notice that this grid is different from the previous one, in which we had *123NNNN* in the bottom row. Here, we divide by *two* factorials, 3! for the *F*'s and 4! for the *N*'s, yielding a much smaller number:

$$\frac{7!}{3! \times 4!} = \frac{7 \times 6 \times 5 \times 4 \times 3 \times 2 \times 1}{(3 \times 2 \times 1) \times (4 \times 3 \times 2 \times 1)} = 7 \times 5 = 35$$

Check Your Skills

5. Peggy will choose 5 of her 8 friends to join her for intramural volleyball. In how many ways can she do so?

Answer can be found on page 107.

Multiple Arrangements

So far, our discussion of combinatorics has revolved around two major topics: (1) the Fundamental Counting Principle and its implications for successive choices, and (2) the anagram approach. The GRE will often *combine* these two ideas on more difficult combinatorics problems, requiring you to choose successive or **multiple arrangements**.

If a GRE problem requires you to choose two or more sets of items from separate pools, count the arrangements <u>separately</u>—perhaps using a different anagram grid each time. Then multiply the numbers of possibilities for each step.

Distinguish these problems—which require choices from *separate pools*—from complex problems that are still single arrangements (all items chosen from the *same pool*). For instance, a problem requiring the choice of a treasurer, a secretary, and three more representatives from <u>one</u> class of 20 students may seem like two or more separate problems, but it is just one: an anagram of one *T*, one *S*, three *R*'s, and fifteen *N*'s in one 20-letter "word."

> The I Eta Pi fraternity must choose a delegation of three senior members and two junior members for an annual interfraternity conference. If I Eta Pi has 12 senior members and 11 junior members, how many different delegations are possible?

This problem involves two genuinely different arrangements: three seniors chosen from a pool of 12 seniors, and two juniors chosen from a *separate* pool of 11 juniors. These arrangements should be calculated separately.

Because the three spots in the delegation are not distinguishable, choosing the seniors is equivalent to choosing an anagram of three Y's and nine N's, which can be accomplished in $\dfrac{12!}{9! \times 3!} = 220$ different ways. Similarly, choosing the juniors is equivalent to choosing an anagram of two Y's and nine N's, which can be done in $\dfrac{11!}{9! \times 2!} = 55$ different ways.

Since the choices are successive and independent, multiply the numbers: $220 \times 55 = 12{,}100$ different delegations are possible.

Check Your Skills

6. Three men (out of 7) and three women (out of 6) will be chosen to serve on a committee. In how many ways can the committee be formed?

Answer can be found on page 107.

Check Your Skills Answers

1. **12:** Multiply the number of choices for each leg of the trip: $3 \times 4 = 12$.

2. **18:** John has 3 choices of pants, 3 choices of shirts and 2 choices involving a tie (yes or no). His total number of choices is $3 \times 2 \times 2 = 18$.

3. **120:** This question is asking for the number of ways to order 5 colored rings with no restrictions.

$5! = \underline{5} \times \underline{4} \times \underline{3} \times \underline{2} \times \underline{1} = 120.$

4. **5,040:** A 7-letter word with all distinct letters has $7! = 5{,}040$ anagrams.

5. **56:** Produce an Anagram Grid using 1 through 8 for the friends, Y for Yes (i.e., joining Peggy), and N for No (not joining Peggy):

Friend	1	2	3	4	5	6	7	8
Status	Y	Y	Y	Y	Y	N	N	N

Anagram the "word" $YYYYYNNN$: $\dfrac{8!}{5!3!} = \dfrac{8 \times 7 \times 6 \times 5 \times 4 \times 3 \times 2 \times 1}{(5 \times 4 \times 3 \times 2 \times 1) \times (3 \times 2 \times 1)} = \dfrac{8 \times 7 \times 6}{3 \times 2 \times 1} = 56$

6. **700:** For the men, anagram the word $YYYNNNN$: $\dfrac{7!}{3!4!} = \dfrac{7 \times 6 \times 5 \times 4 \times 3 \times 2 \times 1}{(3 \times 2 \times 1)(4 \times 3 \times 2 \times 1)} = \dfrac{7 \times 6 \times 5}{3 \times 2 \times 1} = 35$

For the women, anagram the word $YYYNNN$: $\dfrac{6!}{3!3!} = \dfrac{6 \times 5 \times 4 \times 3 \times 2 \times 1}{(3 \times 2 \times 1)(3 \times 2 \times 1)} = \dfrac{6 \times 5 \times 4}{3 \times 2 \times 1} = 20$

Multiply the choices to get the total: $35 \times 20 = 700$ ways. (This is considerably fewer than the number of ways to choose 6 out of 13 people without regard to gender.)

Problem Set

Solve the following problems, using the strategies you have learned in this section.

1. In how many different ways can the letters in the word "LEVEL" be arranged?

2. Amy and Adam are making boxes of truffles to give out as wedding favors. They have an unlimited supply of 5 different types of truffles. If each box holds 2 truffles of different types, how many different boxes can they make?

3. A men's basketball league assigns every player a two-digit number for the back of his jersey. If the league uses only the digits 1–5, what is the maximum number of players that can join the league such that no player has a number with a repeated digit (e.g. 22), and no two players have the same number?

4. A pod of 6 dolphins always swims single file, with 3 females at the front and 3 males in the rear. In how many different arrangements can the dolphins swim?

5. A delegation from Gotham City goes to Metropolis to discuss a limited Batman–Superman partnership. If the mayor of Metropolis chooses 3 members of the 7-person delegation to meet with Superman, how many different 3-person combinations can he choose?

6. Mario's Pizza has two choices of crust: deep dish and thin-and-crispy. The restaurant also has a choice of 5 toppings: tomatoes, sausage, peppers, onions, and pepperoni. Finally, Mario's offers every pizza in extra-cheese as well as regular. If Linda's volleyball team decides to order a pizza with four toppings, how many different choices do the teammates have at Mario's Pizza?

7.

Country X has a four-digit postal code assigned to each town, such that the first digit is non-zero, and none of the digits is repeated.

Quantity A	**Quantity B**
The number of possible postal codes in Country X	4,500

8.

8 athletes compete in a race in which a gold, a silver and a bronze medal will be awarded to the top three finishers, in that order.

Quantity A	**Quantity B**
The number of ways in which the medals can be awarded	$8 \times 3!$

9.

Lothar has 6 stamps from Utopia and 4
stamps from Cornucopia in his collection.
He will give two stamps of each type to his
friend Peggy Sue.

Quantity A   **Quantity B**

The number of ways Lothar
can give four stamps (two of   100
each type) to Peggy Sue

1. **30:** There are two repeated E's and two repeated L's in the word "*LEVEL*." To find the anagrams for this word, set up a fraction in which the numerator is the factorial of the number of letters and the denominator is the factorial of the number of each repeated letter.

$$\frac{5!}{2!2!} = \frac{5 \times 4 \times 3 \times 2 \times 1}{2 \times 1 \times 2 \times 1} = 30$$

Alternatively, you can solve this problem using the Slot Method, as long as you correct for over-counting (since you have some indistinguishable elements). There are five choices for the first letter, four for the second, and so on, making the product $5 \times 4 \times 3 \times 2 \times 1 = 120$. However, there are two sets of 2 indistinguishable elements each, so you must divide by 2! to account for each of these. Thus, the total number of combinations is $\frac{5 \times 4 \times 3 \times 2 \times 1}{2! \times 2!} = 30$.

2. **10:** In every combination, two types of truffles will be in the box, and three types of truffles will not. Therefore, this problem is a question about the number of anagrams that can be made from the "word" *YYNNN*:

$$\frac{5!}{2!3!} = \frac{5 \times 4 \times 3 \times 2 \times 1}{3 \times 2 \times 1 \times 2 \times 1} = 5 \times 2 = 10$$

A	B	C	D	E
Y	Y	N	N	N

This problem can also be solved with the formula for combinations, since it is a combination of two items chosen from a set of five (in which order does not matter). Therefore, there are $\frac{5!}{2! \times 3!} = 10$ possible combinations.

3. **20:** In this problem, the order of the numbers matters. Each number can be either the tens digit, the units digit, or not a digit in the number. Therefore, this problem is a question about the number of anagrams that can be made from the "word" *TUNNN*:

$$\frac{5!}{3!} = \frac{5 \times 4 \times 3 \times 2 \times 1}{3 \times 2 \times 1} = 5 \times 4 = 20$$

1	2	3	4	5
T	U	N	N	N

This problem can also be solved with the formula for permutations. The situation is a permutation of two items chosen from a set of five (order matters this time, since switching the two digits produces a genuinely different jersey number).

Therefore, there are $\frac{5!}{(5-2)!} = \frac{5!}{3!} = 20$ possible permutations. (Remember, in the permutation formula, you always divide, not by the factorial of the number chosen, but by the factorial of the number NOT chosen.)

You can also use the slot method. The slots correspond to the positions of the digits (tens and units). You have 5 choices for the tens digit and then only 4 choices for the units digit (since you cannot use the same digit again), resulting in $5 \times 4 = 20$ possibilities. This method works well for problems in which order matters.

Finally, you can just list out the jersey numbers, since the number of possibilities is low. Even if you stop partway through, this can be a good way to start, so that you get a sense of the problem.

12, 13, 14, 15, 21, 23, 24, 25, 31, 32, 34, 35, 41, 42, 43, 45, 51, 52, 53, 54 = 5 groups of 4 = 20.

4. **36:** There are 3! ways in which the 3 females can swim. There are 3! ways in which the 3 males can swim. Therefore, there are $3! \times 3!$ ways in which the entire pod can swim:

$3! \times 3! = 6 \times 6 = 36.$

This is a multiple arrangements problem, in which we have 2 separate pools (females and males).

5. **35:** Model this problem with anagrams for the "word" *YYYNNNN*, in which three people are in the delegation and 4 are not:

$$\frac{7!}{3!4!} = \frac{7 \times 6 \times 5}{3 \times 2 \times 1} = 35$$ Note that you must divide by both 3! and 4! in this problem.

Alternatively, you can use the combination formula, because this problem requires the number of possible combinations of 3 delegates taken from a total of 7. (Note that order does not matter.) Therefore, the number of possible

combinations is $\frac{7!}{3! \times 4!} = 35$.

A	B	C	D	E	F	G
Y	Y	Y	N	N	N	N

6. **20:** Consider the toppings first. Model the toppings with the "word" *YYYYN*, in which four of the toppings are on the pizza and one is not. The number of anagrams for this "word" is:

A	B	C	D	E
Y	Y	Y	Y	N

$$\frac{5!}{4!} = 5$$

If each of these pizzas can also be offered in 2 choices of crust, there are 5 × 2 = 10 pizzas. The same logic applies for extra-cheese and regular: 10 × 2 = 20.

Alternatively, use the combinations formula to count the combinations of toppings: $\frac{5!}{4! \times 1!} = 5$. Or use an intuitive

approach: choosing four toppings out of five is equivalent to choosing the ONE topping that will not be on the

pizza. There are clearly 5 ways to do that.

7. **A:** We can use the Slot Method to solve this problem. The first slot can be filled by any one of the digits from 1 through 9, since 0 is disallowed. The second digit has no restriction involving zero; however, the digit that was used in the first slot may not be reused. Thus the second slot also has nine possibilities. The third and fourth slots may not use previously used digits, so they may be filled with 8 and 7 different digits, respectively. The total number of possible postal codes is therefore:

$$9 \times 9 \times 8 \times 7 = 4{,}536$$

Country X has a four-digit postal code assigned to each town, such that the first digit is non-zero, and none of the digits is repeated.

Quantity A	**Quantity B**
The number of possible postal codes in Country X = **4,536**	4,500

Therefore **Quantity A is greater.**

8. **A:** The Anagram Grid is a good method for solving this problem. We can use the numbers 1 through 8 to uniquely designate each athlete. In the second row, G, S and B designate the three medals, while the athletes who get no medal can each be associated with an N:

Athlete	1	2	3	4	5	6	7	8
Medal	G	S	B	N	N	N	N	N

The number of ways the medals can be awarded is the number of ways the "word" *GSBNNNNN* can be anagrammed. Because 5 of the letters are repeated, the answer is given by $\dfrac{8!}{5!} = \dfrac{8 \times 7 \times 6 \times 5 \times 4 \times 3 \times 2 \times 1}{5 \times 4 \times 3 \times 2 \times 1} = 8 \times 7 \times 6.$

Compare this number to $8 \times 3!$.

$$8 \times 3! = 8 \times 3 \times 2 \times 1 = 8 \times 6.$$

Rewrite the quantities:

Quantity A	**Quantity B**
The number of ways in which the medals can be awarded = **$8 \times 7 \times 6$**	$8 \times 3! = \mathbf{8 \times 6}$

Therefore **Quantity A is larger.**

9. **B:** This exercise can be regarded as two successive "pick a group" problems. First, Lothar picks 2 out of 6 Utopian stamps, and then 2 out of 4 Cornucopian stamps. Each selection may be computed according to the general formula $\dfrac{\text{Pool!}}{(\text{In! Out!})}$. The two numbers thus obtained must then be multiplied to give the final result:

$$\text{Total number of ways } = \left(\frac{6!}{2!4!}\right) \times \left(\frac{4!}{2!2!}\right) = \left(\frac{6 \times 5}{2 \times 1}\right) \times \left(\frac{4 \times 3}{2 \times 1}\right) = 15 \times 6 = 90$$

Quantity A	**Quantity B**
The number of ways Lothar can give four stamps (two of each type) to Peggy Sue = **90**	**100**

Therefore **Quantity B is larger.**

Chapter 7
of
WORD PROBLEMS

PROBABILITY

In This Chapter . . .

- "1" is the Greatest Probability

- More Than One Event: "AND" vs. "OR"

- The "$1 - x$" Probability Trick

- The Domino Effect

PROBABILITY

Probability is a quantity that expresses the chance, or likelihood, of an event. In other words, it measures how often an event will occur in a long series of repeated trials.

For events with countable outcomes, probability is defined by the following fraction:

$$\text{Probability} = \frac{\text{Number of \textit{desired} or \textit{successful} outcomes}}{\text{Total number of \textit{possible} outcomes}}$$

This fraction assumes all *outcomes are equally likely*. If not, the math can be more complicated (more on this later.)

As a simple illustration, rolling a die (singular for dice) has **six** possible outcomes: 1, 2, 3, 4, 5, and 6. The probability of rolling a "5" is 1/6, because the "5" corresponds to only **one** of those outcomes. The probability of rolling a prime number, though, is 3/6 = 1/2, because in that case, three of the outcomes (2, 3, and 5) are considered successes.

Again, all the outcomes must be equally likely. One might say, for instance, that the lottery has only two "outcomes"—win or lose—but that does not mean the probability of winning the lottery is 1/2. If you want to calculate the correct probability of winning the lottery, you must find *all of the possible equally likely outcomes*. In other words, you have to count up all the specific combinations of differently numbered balls in the lottery to determine the correct probability of winning the lottery.

In most problems, you will have to think carefully about how to break a situation down into equally likely outcomes. Consider the following problem:

> If a fair coin is tossed three times, what is the probability that it will turn up heads exactly twice?

You may be tempted to say that there are four possibilities—no heads, 1 head, 2 heads, and 3 heads—and that the probability of 2 heads is thus 1/4. You would be wrong, though, because those four outcomes are not equally likely. You are much more likely to get 1 or 2 heads than to get all heads or all tails. Instead, you have to formulate equally likely outcomes in terms of the outcome of each flip:

HHH HHT HTH THH HTT THT TTH TTT

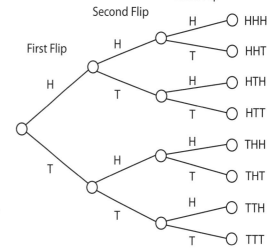

If you have trouble formulating this list from scratch, you can use a **counting tree**, which breaks down possible outcomes step by step, with only one decision at each branch of the tree. An example is shown to the right.

These eight outcomes are equally likely, because the coin is equally likely to come up heads or tails at each flip. Three outcomes on this list (HHT, HTH, THH) have heads exactly twice, so the probability of exactly two heads is 3/8.

This result can also be written thus:

P(exactly 2 heads) = 3/8.

"1" is the Greatest Probability

The greatest probability—the *certainty* that an event will occur—is 1. Thus, a probability of 1 means that the event must occur. For example:

The probability that you roll a fair die once, and it lands on a number less than seven, is certain, or 1.

$$\frac{\text{Number of } \textit{successful} \text{ outcomes}}{\text{Total number of possible outcomes}} = \frac{6}{6} = 1$$

As a percent, this certainty is expressed as 100%.

The lowest probability—the *impossibility* that an event will occur—is 0. Thus, a probability of 0 means that an event will NOT occur. For example, the probability that you roll a fair die once and it lands on the number 9 is impossible—a probability of 0.

$$\frac{\text{Number of } \textit{successful} \text{ outcomes}}{\text{Total number of possible outcomes}} = \frac{0}{6} = 0$$

As a percent, this impossibility is expressed as 0%.

Thus, probabilities can also be expressed as percents between 0% and 100%, inclusive, or fractions between 0 and 1, inclusive.

More than One Event: "AND" vs. "OR"

Probability problems that deal with multiple events usually involve two primary operations: multiplication and addition. The key to understanding probability is to understand *when you must multiply* and *when you must add.*

1) Assume that X and Y are <u>independent</u> events. **To determine the probability that event X AND event Y will both occur, MULTIPLY the two probabilities together.** Note that the events <u>must</u> be independent for this to work!

> What is the probability that a fair coin flipped twice will land on heads both times?

This is an "AND" problem, because it is asking for the probability that the coin will land on heads on the first flip AND on the second flip. The probability that the coin will land on heads on the first flip is 1/2. The probability that the coin will land on heads on the second flip is 1/2. These events <u>are</u> independent of each other.

Therefore, the probability that the coin will land on heads on both flips is $\frac{1}{2} \times \frac{1}{2} = \frac{1}{4}$.

Note that the probability of having BOTH flips come up heads (1/4) is less than the probability of just one flip come up heads (1/2). This should make intuitive sense. If you define success in a more constrained way (e.g., "to win, BOTH this AND that have to happen"), then the probability of success will be lower. The operation of multiplication should also make sense. Typical probabilities are fractions between 0 and 1. When you multiply together two such fractions, you get a *smaller* result, which means a lower probability.

2) Assume that X and Y are <u>mutually exclusive</u> events (meaning that the two events cannot both occur). **To determine the probability that event X OR event Y will occur, ADD the two probabilities together.**

What is the probability that a fair die rolled once will land on <u>either</u> 4 or 5?

This is an "OR" problem, because it is asking for the probability that the die will land on either 4 **or** 5. The probability that the die will land on 4 is 1/6. The probability that the die will land on 5 is 1/6. The two outcomes are mutually exclusive: the die cannot land on BOTH 4 and 5 at the same time.

Therefore, the probability that the die will land on either 4 or 5 is $\dfrac{1}{6} + \dfrac{1}{6} = \dfrac{2}{6} = \dfrac{1}{3}$.

Note that the probability of having the die come up either 4 or 5 (1/3) is greater than the probability of a 4 by itself (1/6) or of a 5 by itself (1/6). This should make intuitive sense. If you define success in a less constrained way (e.g., "I can win EITHER this way OR that way"), then the probability of success will be higher. The operation of addition should also make sense. Typical probabilities are fractions between 0 and 1. When you add together two such fractions, you get a *larger* result, which means a higher probability.

Note that for adding "OR" probabilities, up until now we have assumed that the events are <u>mutually exclusive</u> (meaning that both events cannot occur). What happens if the events are <u>*not*</u> mutually exclusive?

If that is the case and we simply add the probabilities, we will be double-counting the instances when <u>both</u> events occur. Thus, we must <u>subtract out</u> the probability that both events occur.

If events X and Y are not mutually exclusive, then $P(X \underline{\text{ OR }} Y) = P(X) + P(Y) - P(X \underline{\text{ AND }} Y)$.

> Suppose a box contains 20 balls. Ten balls are white and marked with the integers 1–10. The other ten balls are red and marked with the integers 11–20. If one ball is selected, what is the probability that the ball will be white <u>or</u> will be marked with an even number?

Since half the balls are white and half are marked with an even number $P(\text{white}) + P(\text{even})$ would give us $\dfrac{1}{2} + \dfrac{1}{2} = 1$.

This is <u>incorrect</u>! We must subtract out the probability that the ball is <u>both white and marked with an even number.</u> There are 5 such balls out of 20. Thus the correct answer is: $P(\text{white} \underline{\text{ OR }} \text{even}) = P(\text{white}) + P(\text{even}) - P(\text{white}$ <u>AND</u> even$) = \dfrac{1}{2} + \dfrac{1}{2} - \dfrac{5}{20} = 1 - \dfrac{1}{4} = \dfrac{3}{4}$.

Check Your Skills

1. If a die is rolled twice, what is the probability that it will land on an even number both times?
2. Eight runners in a race are equally likely to win the race. What is the probability that the race will be won by the runner in lane 1 or the runner in lane 8?
3. A fair die is rolled and a fair coin is flipped. What is the probability that either the die will come up 2 or 3, <u>or</u> the coin will land heads up?

Answers can be found on page 123.

The "1 − x" Probability Trick

As shown in the previous section, you can solve "OR" problems (explicit or disguised) by combining the probabilities of individual events. If there are many individual events, though, such calculation may be tedious and time-consuming. The good news is that you may not have to perform these calculations. In certain types of "OR" problems, the probability of the desired event NOT happening may be much easier to calculate.

For example, in the previous section, we could have calculated the probability of getting at least one head on two flips by considering how we would NOT get at least one head. However, it would not be too much work to compute the probability directly, using the slightly more complicated "OR" formula.

But let us say that a salesperson makes five sales calls, and you want to find the likelihood that he or she makes <u>at least</u> one sale. If you try to calculate this probability directly, you will have to confront five separate possibilities that constitute "success": exactly 1 sale, exactly 2 sales, exactly 3 sales, exactly 4 sales, or exactly 5 sales. It would seem that you would have no choice but to calculate each of those probabilities separately and then add them together. This will be far too much work, especially under timed conditions.

However, consider the probability of *failure*—that is, the salesperson *does not* make at least one sale. Now you have only one possibility to consider: zero sales. You can now calculate the probability in which you are interested, because for *any* event, the following relationship is true:

Probability of SUCCESS + Probability of FAILURE = 1
(the event happens)   (it does not happen)

*If on a GRE problem, "success" contains **multiple possibilities**—especially if the wording contains phrases such as "at least" and "at most"—then consider finding the probability that success **does not happen**. If you can find this "failure" probability more easily (call it x), then the probability you really want to find will be **1 − x**.*

For example:

> What is the probability that, on three rolls of a single fair die, AT LEAST ONE of the rolls will be a six?

We could list all the possible outcomes of three rolls of a die (1–1–1, 1–1–2, 1–1–3, etc.), and then determine how many of them have at least one six, but this would be very time-consuming. Instead, it is easier to think of this problem in reverse before solving.

> <u>Failure</u>: What is the probability that <u>NONE</u> of the rolls will yield a 6?

On each roll, there is a $\dfrac{5}{6}$ probability that the die will <u>not</u> yield a 6.

Thus, the probability that on all 3 rolls the die will <u>not</u> yield a 6 is $\dfrac{5}{6} \times \dfrac{5}{6} \times \dfrac{5}{6} = \dfrac{125}{216}$.

Now, we originally defined success as rolling at least one six. Since we have found the probability of failure, we answer the original question by subtracting this probability from 1:

$1 - \dfrac{125}{216} = \dfrac{91}{216}$ is the probability that at least one six will be rolled.

Check Your Skills

4. If a die is rolled twice, what is the probability that it will land on an even number at least once?
Answers can be found on page 123.

The Domino Effect

Sometimes the outcome of the first event will affect the probability of a subsequent event. For example:

> In a box with 10 blocks, 3 of which are red, what is the probability of picking out a red block on each of your first two tries? Assume that you do NOT replace the first block after you have picked it.

Since this is an "AND" problem, we must find the probability of both events and multiply them together. Consider how easy it is to make the following mistake:

You compute the probability of picking a red block on your first pick as $\dfrac{3}{10}$.

You compute the probability of picking a red block on your second pick as $\dfrac{3}{10}$.

So you compute the probability of picking a red block on both picks as $\dfrac{3}{10} \times \dfrac{3}{10} = \dfrac{9}{100}$.

This solution is WRONG, because it does not take into account that the first event affects the second event. If a red block is chosen on the first pick, then the number of blocks now in the box has decreased from **10 to 9**. Additionally, the number of red blocks now in the box has decreased from **3 to 2**. Therefore, the probability of choosing a red block on the second pick is different from the probability of choosing a red block on the first pick.

The CORRECT solution to this problem is as follows:

The probability of picking a red block on your first pick is $\dfrac{3}{10}$.

The probability of picking a red block on your second pick is $\dfrac{2}{9}$.

Therefore, the probability of picking a red block on both picks is $\dfrac{3}{10} \times \dfrac{2}{9} = \dfrac{6}{90} = \dfrac{1}{15}$.

Do not forget to analyze events by considering whether one event affects subsequent events. The first roll of a die or flip of a coin has no effect on any subsequent rolls or flips. However, the first pick of an object out of a box _does_ affect subsequent picks if you do not replace that object. This scenario is called "no replacement" or "without replacement."

If you <u>are</u> supposed to replace the object, the problem should clearly tell you so. In this scenario (called "with replacement"), the first pick does not affect the second pick.

Check Your Skills

5. A drawer contains 7 white shirts and 3 red shirts. What is the probability of picking a white shirt, followed by a red shirt if the first shirt is not put back in?

Answers can be found on page 123.

Check Your Skills Answers

1. **1/4:** For each throw, the probability of an even number is $3/6 = 1/2$. We multiply the individual probabilities because the two outcomes are independent: $P = 1/2 \times 1/2 = 1/4$.

2. **1/4:** $P(1) = 1/8$, $P(8) = 1/8$, $P(1 \text{ or } 8) = 1/8 + 1/8 = 1/4$.

3. **2/3:** $P(2 \text{ or } 3) = 1/6 + 1/6 = 1/3$, $P(\text{Heads}) = 1/2$ and $P(\text{Both}) = 1/3 \times 1/2$ (because the die roll and coin flip are independent events). Thus $P(2 \text{ OR } 3 \text{ OR Heads}) = 1/3 + 1/2 - 1/6 = 2/3$.

4. **3/4:** If the die does not land on an even number at least once, then it must have landed on an odd number both times. For each throw, the probability of an odd number is $3/6 = 1/2$. Multiply the individual probabilities to get the probability of two odd numbers in a row: $x = 1/2 \times 1/2 = 1/4$. Then the probability of at least one even number is $1 - x = 1 - 1/4 = 3/4$.

5. **7/30:** There are 10 shirts total.

    Probability of picking a white shirt first: $7/10$.

    Probability of picking a red shirt next (out of 9 remaining): $3/9 = 1/3$.

    Probability of picking white first, then red: $7/10 \times 3/9 = 21/90 = 7/30$.

Problem Set

Solve the following problems. Express probabilities as fractions or percentages unless otherwise instructed.

1.   What is the probability that the sum of two dice will yield a 4 or 6?

2.   What is the probability that the sum of two dice will yield anything but an 8?

3.   What is the probability that the sum of two dice will yield a 7, and then when both are thrown again, their sum will again yield a 7?

4.   What is the probability that the sum of two dice will yield a 5, and then when both are thrown again, their sum will yield a 9?

5.   At a certain pizzeria, 1/6 of the pizzas sold in a week were cheese, and 1/5 of the OTHER pizzas sold were pepperoni. If Brandon bought a randomly chosen pizza from the pizzeria that week, what is the probability that he ordered a pepperoni?

6.   John invites 12 friends to a dinner party, half of which are men. Exactly one man and one woman are bringing desserts. If one person from this group is selected at random, what is the probability that it is a woman, or a man who is not bringing a dessert?

7.

A fair coin is flipped 5 times.

Quantity A	**Quantity B**
The probability of getting more heads than tails	1/2

8.

A jar contains 3 red and 2 white marbles. Two marbles are picked without replacement.

Quantity A	**Quantity B**
The probability of picking two red marbles	The probability of picking exactly one red and one white marble

9.

A die is rolled n times, where n is at least 3.

Quantity A	**Quantity B**
The probability that at least one of the throws yields a 6	1/2

1. **2/9:** There are 36 ways in which 2 dice can be thrown ($6 \times 6 = 36$). The combinations that yield sums of 4 and 6 are $1 + 3$, $2 + 2$, $3 + 1$, $1 + 5$, $2 + 4$, $3 + 3$, $4 + 2$, and $5 + 1$: 8 different combinations. Therefore, the probability is 8/36, or 2/9.

2. **31/36:** Solve this problem by calculating the probability that the sum WILL yield a sum of 8, and then subtract the result from 1. There are 5 combinations of 2 dice that yield a sum of 8: $2 + 6$, $3 + 5$, $4 + 4$, $5 + 3$, and $6 + 2$. (Note that $7 + 1$ is not a valid combination, as there is no 7 on a standard die.) Therefore, the probability that the sum will be 8 is 5/36, and the probability that the sum will NOT be 8 is $1 - 5/36$, or 31/36.

3. **1/36:** There are 36 ways in which 2 dice can be thrown ($6 \times 6 = 36$). The combinations that yield a sum of 7 are $1 + 6$, $2 + 5$, $3 + 4$, $4 + 3$, $5 + 2$, and $6 + 1$: 6 different combinations. Therefore, the probability of rolling a 7 is 6/36, or 1/6. To find the probability that this will happen twice in a row, multiply 1/6 by 1/6 to get 1/36.

4. **1/81:** First, find the individual probability of each event. The probability of rolling a 5 is 4/36, or 1/9, since there are 4 ways to roll a sum of 5 ($1 + 4$, $2 + 3$, $3 + 2$, and $4 + 1$). The probability of rolling a 9 is also 4/36, or 1/9, since there are 4 ways to roll a sum of 9 ($3 + 6$, $4 + 5$, $5 + 4$, and $6 + 3$). To find the probability that both events will happen in succession, multiply $1/9 \times 1/9$: 1/81.

5. **1/6:** If 1/6 of the pizzas were cheese, 5/6 of the pizzas were not. 1/5 of these 5/6 were pepperoni. Multiply to find the total portion: $1/5 \times 5/6 = 1/6$. If 1/6 of the pizzas were pepperoni, there is a 1/6 chance that Brandon bought a pepperoni pizza.

6. $\dfrac{\mathbf{11}}{\mathbf{12}}$: $P(\text{woman}) = \dfrac{6}{12} = \dfrac{1}{2}$

$P(\text{not bringing a dessert}) = \dfrac{10}{12} = \dfrac{5}{6}$

$P(\text{woman \underline{and} not bringing a dessert}) = \dfrac{1}{2} \times \dfrac{5}{6} = \dfrac{5}{12}$

$P(\text{woman \underline{or} a man not bringing a dessert}) = \dfrac{1}{2} + \dfrac{5}{6} - \dfrac{5}{12} = \dfrac{6 + 10 - 5}{12} = \dfrac{11}{12}.$

Alternatively, we could note that 6 women are invited and 5 men <u>who are not bringing a dessert</u> are invited. Thus $6 + 5 = 11$ out of 12 would fit the description.

7. **C:** Because heads and tails are equally likely, it follows that the probability of getting more heads than tails should be exactly the same as the probability of getting more tails than heads. The only remaining option is that we might get equally many heads and tails. However, because the total number of coin flips is an odd number, the latter is impossible. Therefore the probability of getting more heads than tails must be exactly 1/2. (It is, of course, also possible to compute this probability directly by considering the cases of getting 5, 4 or 3 heads separately. However, this approach would be very time-consuming.)

Another way of thinking about it is that, for every set of flips that has more heads than tails, there is a corresponding set of flips, in which every flip gets the opposite result, that has more tails. For instance, the sequence of throws *HHHHH* is balanced by the sequence *TTTTT*. The sequence *HHHHT* is balanced by the sequence *TTTTH*.

Therefore **the two quantities are equal.**

8. **B:** First, compute the probability of picking two red marbles. This is given by:

$$P(RR) = \frac{3}{5} \times \frac{2}{4} = \frac{3}{10}.$$

Next, consider the probability of picking a red marble followed by a white marble:

$$P(RW) = \frac{3}{5} \times \frac{2}{4} = \frac{3}{10}.$$

However, this is not the only way to pick one red and one white marble; we could have picked the white one first, followed by the red one:

$$P(WR) = \frac{2}{5} \times \frac{3}{4} = \frac{3}{10}.$$

This event is mutually exclusive from picking a red marble followed by a white marble. Thus, the total probability of picking one red and one white marble is the sum of the probabilities of *RW* and *WR*, yielding an answer of:

$$P(RW \text{ or } WR) = \frac{3}{10} + \frac{3}{10} = 2 \times \left(\frac{3}{10}\right) = \frac{6}{10} = \frac{3}{5}.$$

<table>
<tr><td align="center">**Quantity A**</td><td align="center">**Quantity B**</td></tr>
<tr><td align="center">The probability of picking two red marbles = **3/10**</td><td align="center">The probability of picking one red and one white marble = **3/5**</td></tr>
</table>

Therefore **Quantity B is greater.**

9. **D:** The easiest way to compute the probability in question is through the "1 − x" shortcut. To do so, we imagine the opposite of the event of interest, namely, that <u>none</u> of the *n* throws yields a 6. The probability of a single throw not yielding a 6 is 5/6, and because each throw is independent, the cumulative probability of none of the *n* throws yielding a 6 is found by multiplication:

$$P(\text{No 6 in } n \text{ throws}) = \left(\frac{5}{6}\right)^n$$

Powers of fractions less than one get smaller as the exponent increases. Thus, we can see that this probability will become very small for large values of n, such that the probability of getting at least one 6 (which is $1 - \left(\dfrac{5}{6}\right)^n$) will come closer and closer to 1. Thus as n increases, it becomes more and more certain that a 6 will be thrown. The question now is, what is the smallest that the probability of getting at least one six could be? To answer that question, we should let n assume its extreme value, which is 3. In that case the probability of never getting a 6 is given by:

$$P(\text{No 6 in three throws}) = \left(\frac{5}{6}\right)^3 = \frac{125}{216}$$

such that the probability of getting at least one 6 in three throws is given by:

$$P(\text{At least one 6 in three throws}) = 1 - \frac{125}{216} = \frac{91}{216}$$

This value is less than 1/2. As we saw earlier, however, as n grows, it becomes ever more likely that at least one throw will yield a 6, so that the probability eventually surpasses 1/2. Thus Quantity A can be less than or greater than 1/2. **We do not have enough information** to determine which quantity is greater.

Chapter 8

of

Word Problems

MINOR PROBLEM
TYPES

In This Chapter . . .

- Optimization

- Grouping

- Overlapping Sets

MINOR PROBLEM TYPES

The GRE occasionally contains problems that fall into one of three categories:

    a. *Optimization*: maximizing or minimizing a quantity by choosing optimal values of related quantities.
    b. *Grouping*: putting people or items into different groups to fit some criteria.
    c. *Overlapping sets:* people or items who can belong in one of two groups, neither, or both.

You should approach all three of these problem types with the same general outlook, although it is unlikely that you will see more than one of them on the same administration of the GRE. The general approach is to focus on **extreme scenarios**.

You should mind the following three considerations when considering any grouping or optimization problem:
    1. Be aware of both ***explicit constraints*** (restrictions actually stated in the text) and ***hidden constraints*** (restrictions implied by the real-world aspects of a problem). For instance, in a problem requiring the separation of 40 people into 6 groups, hidden constraints require the number of people in each group to be a positive whole number.
    2. In most cases, you can maximize or minimize quantities (or optimize schedules, etc.) by ***choosing the highest or lowest values*** of the variables that you are allowed to select.
    3. For ***overlapping sets***, remember that people/items who fit in both categories remove people/items in just one category. Thus all other things being equal, the ***more people/items in "both," the fewer in "just one" and the more in "neither."***

Optimization

In general optimization problems, you are asked to maximize or minimize some quantity, given constraints on other quantities. These quantities are all related through some equation.

Consider the following problem:

> The guests at a football banquet consumed a total of 401 pounds of food. If no individual guest consumed more than 2.5 pounds of food, what is the minimum number of guests that could have attended the banquet?

You can visualize the underlying equation in the following table:

Pounds of food per guest	×	Guests	=	Total pounds of food
At MOST 2.5 *maximize*	×	At LEAST ??? *minimize*	=	EXACTLY 401 *constant*

Notice that finding the *minimum* value of the number of guests involves using the *maximum* pounds of food per guest, because the two quantities multiply to a constant. This sort of inversion (i.e. maximizing one thing in order to minimize another) is typical.

Begin by considering the extreme case in which each guest eats as much food as possible, or 2.5 pounds apiece. The corresponding number of guests at the banquet works out to 401/2.5 = 160.4 people.

However, you obviously cannot have a fractional number of guests at the banquet. Thus the answer must be rounded.

To determine whether to round up or down, consider the explicit constraint: the amount of food per guest is a *maximum* of 2.5 pounds per guest. Therefore, the *minimum* number of guests is 160.4 (if guests could be fractional), and we must *round up* to make the number of guests an integer: 161.

Note the careful reasoning required! Although the phrase "*minimum* number of guests" may tempt you to round down, you will get an incorrect answer if you do so. In general, as you solve this sort of problem, put the extreme case into the underlying equation, and solve. Then round appropriately.

Check Your Skills

1. If no one in a group of friends has more than $75, what is the smallest number of people who could be in the group if the group purchases a flat-screen TV that costs $1,100?

Answers can be found on page 137.

Grouping

In grouping problems, you make complete groups of items, drawing these items out of a larger pool. The goal is usually to maximize or minimize some quantity, such as the number of complete groups or the number of leftover items that do not fit into complete groups. As such, these problems are often really a special case of optimization problems. One approach is to determine the **limiting factor** on the number of complete groups. That is, if you need different types of items for a complete group, figure out how many groups you can make with each item, ignoring the other types (as if you had unlimited quantities of those other items). Then compare your results.

> Orange Computers is breaking up its conference attendees into groups. Each group must have exactly one person from Division A, two people from Division B, and three people from Division C. There are 20 people from Division A, 30 people from Division B, and 40 people from Division C at the conference. What is the smallest number of people who will <u>not</u> be able to be assigned to a group?

The first step is to find out how many groups you can make with the people from each division separately, ignoring the other divisions. There are enough Division A people for 20 groups, but only enough Division B people for 15 groups (= 30 people ÷ 2 people per group). As for Division C, there are only enough people for 13 groups, since 40 people ÷ 3 people per group = 13 groups, plus one person left over. So the limiting factor is Division C: only 13 complete groups can be formed. These 13 groups will take up 13 Division A people (leaving 20 − 13 = 7 left over) and 26 Division B people (leaving 30 − 26 = 4 left over). Together with the 1 Division C person left over, 1 + 4 + 7 = 12 people will be left over in total.

For some grouping problems, you may want to think about the **most or least evenly distributed** arrangements of the items. That is, assign items to groups as evenly (or unevenly) as possible to create extreme cases.

Check Your Skills

2. A salad dressing requires oil, vinegar and water in the ratio 2 : 1 : 3. If Oliver has 1 cup of oil, 1/3 cup of vinegar and 2 cups of water, what is the maximum number of cups of dressing that he can mix?

Answers can be found on page 137.

Overlapping Sets

In overlapping sets, people or items will be categorized by their "membership" or "non-membership" in either of <u>two</u> groups. For example, workers in a factory could be salaried or non-salaried. They could also work in an Operations role, or <u>not</u> work in an Operations role. These problems can be represented by a simple Venn diagram, as demonstrated on the next page.

Workers in a Factory

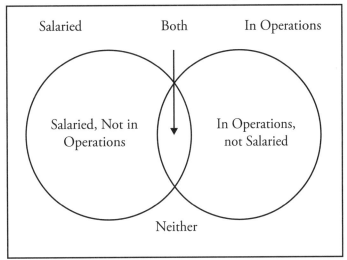

The key points to note are the following:

1. The workers will <u>always</u> fall into one of four groups:

    a) Salaried and in an Operations role (i.e., "both")
    b) Salaried and <u>not</u> in an Operations role
    c) <u>Not</u> salaried and in an Operations role
    d) <u>Not</u> salaried and <u>not</u> in an Operations role

Therefore there are 4 unknowns in this type of problem, generally (although the question itself may only require that you work with 2 or 3 of them).

2. The problem will often give you total amounts for the groups (salaried, and in Operations), and you will have to use logic to figure out whichever unknown the question is asking about.

The various sections can be labeled as follows:

Workers in a Factory: <u>Total</u>

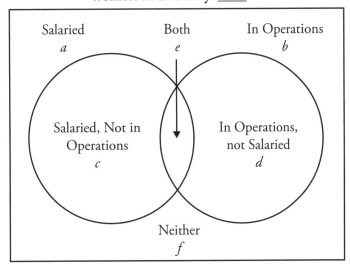

As you can see, $c = a - e$; $d = b - e$, and <u>Total</u> $= a + b - e + f$.

Alternatively, <u>Total</u> $= c + d + e + f$.

Let's make this concrete with an example.

> At Factory X, there are 400 total workers. 240 are salaried, and 200 work in Operations. If at least 100 of the workers are non-salaried and do not work in Operations, what's the minimum number of workers who both are salaried and work in Operations?

Graphically, this looks like:

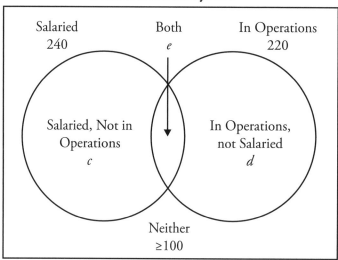

Workers in a Factory: 400

Mathematically, we can use <u>Total</u> $= a + b - e + f$.

$$400 = 240 + 220 - e + (\geq 100)$$
$$e = 240 + 220 - 400 + (\geq 100)$$
$$e = 60 + (\geq 100)$$
$$e = \geq 160$$

Thus at <u>least</u> 160 workers are salaried and work in operations.

Check Your Skills

3. Of 320 consumers, 200 eat strawberries and 300 eat oranges. If all 320 eat at least one of the fruits, how many eat both?

Answers can be found on page 137.

Check Your Skills Answers

1. **15:** The group will be as small as possible when everyone contributes as much as they're able to. The most anyone can contribute is $75, so assume that everyone contributes $75.

$$1,100 \div 75 = 14\frac{2}{3}$$

14 people contributing $75 would only give $1,050. Therefore you need to round up. The smallest number of people that could be in the group is 15.

2. **2 cups:** Try the limits: If Oliver used 1 cup of oil, his recipe would require 1/2 cup of vinegar and 1¹/2 cups of water. He does not have enough vinegar. If he used 1/3 cup of vinegar, he would need 2/3 cups of oil and 1 cup of water, both of which he has. He would then have 2/3 + 1/3 + 1 = 2 cups of dressing. He cannot possibly make more dressing than this, because he does not have any more vinegar.

3. **180:** Graphically:

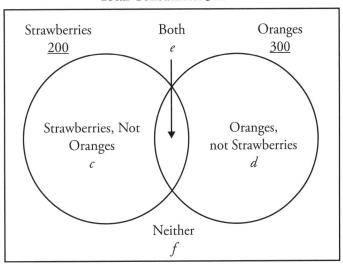

Total Consumers: 320

Mathematically, we can use $\underline{\text{Total}} = a + b - e + f$.

Since all of the consumers eat at least one of the fruits, $f = 0$. So, $320 = 200 + 300 - e + 0$.

$$320 = 500 - e$$
$$e = 180$$

Problem Set

1. Velma has exactly one week to learn all 71 Japanese hiragana characters. If she can learn at most a dozen of them on any one day and will only have time to learn four of them on Friday, what is the least number of hiragana characters that Velma will have to learn on Saturday?

2. Huey's Hip Pizza sells two sizes of square pizzas: a small pizza that measures 10 inches on a side and costs $10, and a large pizza that measures 15 inches on a side and costs $20. If two friends go to Huey's with $30 apiece, how many more square inches of pizza can they buy if they pool their money than if they each purchase pizza alone?

3. An eccentric casino owner decides that his casino should only use chips in $5 and $7 denominations. Which of the following amounts cannot be paid out using these chips?

    (A) $31   (B) $29   (C) $26   (D) $23   (E) $21

4. A "Collector's Coin Set" contains a one dollar coin, a fifty-cent coin, a quarter (= 25 cents), a dime (= 10 cents), a nickel (= 5 cents), and a penny (= 1 cent). The Coin Sets are sold for the combined face price of the currency. If Colin buys as many Coin Sets as he can with the $25 he has, how much change will Colin have left over?

5. A rock band is holding a concert and selling tickets. All of the tickets will either be premium seating <u>or</u> allow back-stage access after the event. They will sell 1,200 premium seating tickets and 500 that will allow back-stage access. If 150 of the tickets will <u>both</u> be premium seating and allow back-stage access, how many total tickets will they sell?

6.

Susan is writing a novel that will be 950 pages long when finished. She can write 10 pages per day on weekdays and 20 pages per day on weekends.

Quantity A	**Quantity B**
The least number of consecutive days it will take Susan to finish her novel	75

7.

Jared has four pennies (one cent), one nickel (five cents) and one dime (ten cents).

Quantity A	**Quantity B**
The number of different cent values that Jared can achieve using one or more of his coins	20

8.

A ribbon 40 inches long is to be cut into three pieces, each of whose lengths is a different integer number of inches.

Quantity A

The least possible length, in inches, of the longest piece

Quantity B

15

9.

A farmer sells vegetables to 180 different customers. 90 of them purchase zucchini and 115 of them purchase cauliflower.

Quantity A

The number of customers who purchased <u>both</u> zucchini and cauliflower

Quantity B

The number of customers that purchased <u>neither</u> zucchini <u>nor</u> cauliflower

1. **7**: To minimize the number of hiragana that Velma will have to learn on Saturday, consider the extreme case in which she learns *as many* hiragana *as possible* on the other days. She learns 4 on Friday, leaving $71 - 4 = 67$ for the other six days of the week. If Velma learns the maximum of 12 hiragana on the other five days (besides Saturday), then she will have $67 - 5(12) = 7$ left for Saturday.

2. **25 square inches**: First, figure the area of each pizza: the small is 100 square inches, and the large is 225 square inches.If the two friends pool their money, they can buy three large pizzas, which have a total area of 675 square inches. If they buy individually, though, then each friend will have to buy one large pizza and one small pizza, so they will only have a total of $2(100 + 225) = 650$ square inches of pizza.

3. **D**: This problem is a Grouping Problem. We have some integer number of 5's and some integer number of 7's. Which of the answer choices cannot be the sum? One efficient way to eliminate choices is first to cross off any multiples of 7 and/or 5: this eliminates Choice E. Now, any other possible sums must have at least one 5 and one 7 in them. So you can subtract off 5's one at a time until you reach a multiple of 7. (It is easier to subtract 5's than 7's, because our number system is base-10.)

Choice A: $31 - 5 = 26$; $26 - 5 = 21$, a multiple of 7; this eliminates A. (In other words, $31 = 3 \times 7 + 2 \times 5$.)
Choice B: $29 - 5 = 24$; $24 - 5 = 19$; $19 - 5 = 14$, a multiple of 7; this eliminates B.
Choice C: $26 - 5 = 21$, a multiple of 7; this eliminates C.

So the answer must be Choice D, 23. We check by successively subtracting 5 and looking for multiples of 7: $23 - 5 = 18$, not a multiple of 7; $18 - 5 = 13$, also not a multiple of 7; $13 - 5 = 8$, not a multiple of 7; and no smaller result will be a multiple of 7 either.

4. **$0.17**: The first step is to compute the value of a complete "Collector's Coin Set": $1.00 + $0.50 + $0.25 + $0.10 + $0.05 + $0.01 = $1.91. Now, you need to divide $1.91 into $25. A natural first move is to multiply by 10: for $19.10, Colin can buy 10 complete sets. Now add $1.91 successively. Colin can buy 11 sets for $21.01, 12 sets for $22.92, and 13 sets for $24.83. There are 17 cents left over.

5. **1,550**: We can use the formula Total $= a + b - e + f$. Since all of the tickets will either be premium seating or allow back-stage access, f will equal zero. Therefore:

$$\text{Total} = 1,200 + 500 - 150 = 1,550.$$

6. **B**: In a week consisting of five workdays and two weekend days, Susan can write:

$$5 \times 10 + 2 \times 20 = 90 \text{ pages}$$

Therefore, in ten consecutive full weeks (i.e., 70 consecutive days), she can write 900 pages of her novel, leaving another 50 pages to be written. The least number of days it would take Susan to write 50 pages is three: two weekend days and one weekday. Thus it is possible for Susan to finish her novel in 73 days. (This assumes that Susan chooses her start day appropriately, so as to take advantage of as many weekends as possible.) Therefore **Quantity B is greater.**

7. **B**: Jared can achieve any amount from 1 cent to 19 cents: 1 to 4 cents using the pennies, 5 cents with the nickel, 6 to 9 cents using the nickel along with the pennies, 10 cents using the dime, 11 to 14 cents using the dime along with the pennies, 15 cents using the dime and the nickel, and 16 to 19 cents using the dime and nickel along with the pennies. Notice that 19 cents requires every coin Jared possesses, meaning that 19 is the largest possible value. That makes 19 possible values. Therefore **Quantity B is greater.**

8. **C:** Minimizing the length of the longest piece is equivalent to maximizing the lengths of the remaining pieces, as long as they are shorter than the longest piece. Suppose that the longest piece were 14 inches long (a choice motivated by wanting to be less than the 15 in Quantity B). That would leave 40 − 14 = 26 inches to be accounted for by the other two pieces.

Because each piece must be a different number of inches long, those pieces cannot each be 13 inches long. This, in turn, implies that one of the two remaining pieces would have to be more than 13 inches long—but then, that piece would be 14 inches long, again violating the constraint that each piece be of a different length. Thus the longest piece must be at least 15 inches long, and the shorter pieces could then be 12 and 13 inches long, for a total of 40 inches. The **two quantities are equal.**

9. **A:** Once again using the formula Total = $a + b - e + f$:

$$180 = 90 + 115 - e + f$$
$$180 = 205 - e + f$$
$$e - f = 25$$

Therefore, there will be 25 <u>more</u> customers that purchased both zucchini and cauliflower than those who purchased neither. **Quantity A is larger.**

Chapter 9

of

WORD PROBLEMS

DRILL SETS

In This Chapter . . .

- Word Problems Drill Sets

Word Problems Drill Sets

DRILL SET 1:

Drill 1: Translate the following statements into equations and/or inequalities:

1. The total amount of money saved equals $2,000.
2. The number of cars is three fewer than the number of trucks.
3. There are twice as many computers as there are printers.
4. John ran twice as far as Mary.
5. There are 35 marbles in the jar, some green and some blue.

Drill 2: Translate the following statements into equations and/or inequalities:

1. Container *A* is three times as big as Container *B*.
2. One half of the students are learning French.
3. Max earned one-third of what Jerome earned.
4. The number of people on the team is four less than three times the number of employees.
5. There are 10 more grapes than apples, and one-fourth as many apples as pears.

DRILL SET 2:

Drill 1: Translate and solve the following problems.

1. There are five more computers in the office than employees. If there are 10 employees in the office, how many computers are there?

2. If −5 is 7 more than *z*, what is *z*/4?

3. Each player on the team is required to purchase a uniform that costs $25. If there are 20 players on the team, what will be the total cost of the uniforms?

4. There are two trees in the front yard of a school. The trees have a combined height of 60 feet, and the taller tree is 3 times the height of the shorter tree. How high is the shorter tree?

5. A clothing store bought a container of 100 shirts for $20. If the store sold all of the shirts at $0.50 per shirt, what is the store's gross profit on the container?

Drill 2: Translate and solve the following problems.

1. A bag of 60 marbles is separated into two groups. If the first group contains 16 more marbles than the second group, how many marbles are in the larger group?

2. Two parking lots can hold a total of 115 cars. The Green lot can hold 35 fewer cars than the Red lot. How many cars can the Red lot hold?

3. At the county fair, two people are competing to see who can eat the most hot dogs. One competitor eats 7 less than the other competitor. If the competitor who eats fewer hot dogs eats 25 hot dogs, how many hot dogs did the two people eat, combined?

4. Ben and Sarah ran a combined 30 kilometers. Ben ran 8 kilometers fewer than Sarah did. How many kilometers did Ben run?

5. A class went to a donut shop, where 13 of the students ate 3 donuts each. The remaining 7 students were hungrier, and ate 8 donuts each. How many total donuts did the class eat?

Drill 3: Translate and solve the following problems.

1. Three friends sit down to eat 14 slices of pizza. If two of the friends eat the same number of slices, and the third eats two more slices than each of the other two, how many slices are eaten by the third friend?

2. A plane leaves Chicago in the morning, and makes three flights before returning. The first flight traveled twice as far as the second flight, and the second flight traveled three times as far as the third flight. If the third flight was 45 miles, how many miles was the first flight?

3. A rubber ball is thrown and bounces twice before it is caught. The first time the ball bounces it goes 5 times as high as the second time it bounces. If the second bounce goes 5 feet high, what is the combined height of the two bounces?

4. A museum tour guide can take 1 class through a museum in 30 minutes. If all classes have 30 students, how many students could go through the museum in 2 hours?

5. A band on a concert tour played 10 concerts. The first concert attracted 100 people, and the last concert attracted six times as many people. If the sixth concert attracted 1/2 as many people as the last concert, how many people were at the sixth concert?

Drill 4: Translate and solve the following problems.

1. Movie theater X charges $6 per ticket, and each movie showing costs the theatre $1,750. If 300 people bought tickets for a certain showing, and the theater averaged $2 in concessions (popcorn, etc.) per ticketholder, what was the theater's profit for that showing?

2. Three health clubs are competing to attract new members. One company runs an ad campaign and recruits 120 new members. The second company runs a similar campaign and recruits 2/3 as many members. The third company recruits 10 more members than the second company. How many new members are recruited by the three companies combined?

3. It costs a certain bicycle factory $10,000 to operate for one month, plus $300 for each bicycle produced during the month. Each of the bicycles sells for a retail price of $700. The gross profit of the factory is measured by total income from sales minus the production costs of the bicycles. If 50 bicycles are produced and sold during the month, what is the factory's gross profit?

4. If a harbor cruise can shuttle 50 people per trip, and each trip takes 3 hours, how long will it take for 350 people to complete the tour?

5. Alfred and Nick cooked a total of 49 pies. If twice the number of pies that Alfred cooked was 14 pies more than the number of pies that Nick cooked, how many pies did Alfred cook?

Drill 5: Translate and solve the following problems.

1. Arnaldo earns $11 for each ticket that he sells, and a bonus of $2 per ticket for each ticket he sells over 100. If Arnaldo was paid $2,400, how many tickets did he sell?

2. Alicia is producing a magazine that costs $3 per magazine to print. In addition, she has to pay $10,500 to her staff to design the issue. If Alicia sells each magazine for $10, how many magazines must she sell to break even?

3. Eleanor's football team has won 3 times as many games as Christina's football team. Christina's football team has won four fewer games than Joanna's team. If Joanna's team won 10 games last year, how many games did Eleanor's team win?

4. The distance between Town X and Town Y is twice the distance between Town X and Town Z. The distance between Town Z and Town W is 2/3 the distance between Town Z and Town X. If the distance between Town Z and Town W is 18 miles, how far is Town X from Town Y?

5. Every week, Renee is paid 40 dollars per hour for the first 40 hours she works, and 80 dollars per hour for each hour she works after the first 40 hours. If she earned $2,000 last week, how many hours did she work?

DRILL SET 3:

Drill 1: Translate and solve the following word problems involving age.

1. Norman is 12 years older than Michael. In 6 years, he will be twice as old as Michael. How old is Norman now?

2. Louise is three times as old as Mary. In 5 years, Louise will be twice as old as Mary. How old is Mary now?

3. Chris is 14 years younger than Sam. In 3 years, Sam will be 3 times as old as Chris. How old is Sam now?

4. Toshi is 7 years older than his brother Kosuke, who is twice as old as their younger sister Junko. If Junko is 8 years old, how old is Toshi?

5. Amar is 30 years younger than Lauri. In 5 years, Lauri will be three times as old as Amar. How old will Lauri be in 10 years?

Drill 2: Translate and solve the following word problems involving averages. For the purpose of these problems "average" means the arithmetic mean.

Remember that $A = \dfrac{S}{n}$, where A = average, n = the number of terms, and S = the sum of the terms.

1. 3 lawyers earn an average of $300 per hour. How much money have they earned in total after they each worked 4 hours?

2. The average of 2, 13 and x is 10. What is x?

3. Last year, Nancy earned twice the amount of money that Janet earned. Kate earned three times the amount Janet earned. If Kate earned $45,000 last year, what was the average salary of the three women?

4. John buys 5 books with an average price of $12. If John then buys another book with a price of $18, what is the average price of the six books?

5. If the average of the five numbers $x - 3$, x, $x + 3$, $x + 4$, and $x + 11$ is 45, what is the value of x?

Drill 3: Translate and solve the following word problems involving rates. Remember that $RT = D$, where $R =$ rate, $T =$ time, and $D =$ distance.

1. Bill drove to the store at a rate of 30 miles per hour. If the store is 90 miles away, how long did it take him to get there?

2. Maria normally walks at a rate of 4 miles per hour. If she walks at one half of her normal rate, how long will it take her to walk 4 miles?

3. A train traveled at a constant rate from New York to Chicago in 9 hours. If the distance between New York and Chicago is 630 miles, how fast was the train going?

4. Randy completed a 12 mile run in 4 hours. If Betty ran 3 miles per hour faster than Randy, how long did it take her to complete the same 12 mile run?

5. A truck uses 1 gallon of gasoline every 15 miles. If the truck travels 3 hours at 60 miles per hour, how many gallons of gasoline will it use?

Drill Set Answers

DRILL SET 1:

Set 1, Drill 1:

1. $m = \$2,000$
2. $c = t - 3$
3. $c = 2p$
4. $j = 2m$ (or $dj = 2dm$)
5. $35 = g + b$

Set 1, Drill 2:

1. $A = 3B$
2. $1/2\ S = F$
3. $M = 1/3J$
4. $t = 3e - 4$
5. $g = a + 10$
   $a = 1/4\ p$

DRILL SET 2:

Set 2, Drill 1:

1. **15 computers:** Let c = number of computers.
   Let e = number of employees.

   $c = e + 5$

   If $e = 10$, then $c = (10) + 5$
   $c = 15$

2. **−3:** $-5 = z + 7$
   $z = -12$
   $z/4 = -3$

3. **$500:** Let u = cost of each uniform.

   Let p = number of players.
   Let C = the total cost of the uniforms.

   $C = u \times p$

   If $p = 20$, and $u = \$25$, then

   $C = (\$25) \times (20) = \$500$

4. **15 feet:** Let s = the height of the shorter tree.
   Let t = the height of the taller tree.

$$s + t = 60$$
$$3s = t$$

$$s + (3s) = 60$$
$$4s = 60$$

$$s = 15$$

5. **$30:** Let p = profit.
   Let r = revenue.
   Let c = cost.

Profit = Revenue − Cost
$$p = r - c$$
$$r = 100 \times \$0.50$$
$$c = \$20$$

$$p = (100 \times \$0.50) - (\$20)$$
$$p = \$50 - \$20 = \$30$$

Set 2, Drill 2:

1. **38 marbles:** Let f = the number of marbles in the first group.
   Let s = the number of marbles in the second group.

$$f + s = 60$$
$$f = s + 16$$
$$(s + 16) + s = 60$$
$$2s + 16 = 60$$
$$2s = 44$$
$$s = 22$$

$$f = (22) + 16 = 38$$

2. **75 cars:** Let g = the number of cars that the Green lot can hold.
Let r = the number of cars that the Red lot can hold.

$$g + r = 115$$
$$g = r - 35$$

$$(r - 35) + r = 115$$
$$2r - 35 = 115$$
$$2r = 150$$
$$r = 75$$

$$g = r - 35 = 75 - 35 = 40$$

Red lot: 75 cars
Green lot: 40 cars

3. **57 hot dogs:** Let f = the number of hot dogs eaten by the first competitor (assume he or she ate fewer).
Let s = the number of hot dogs eaten by the second competitor.

$$f = s - 7$$
$$f = 25$$

Therefore,

$$(25) = s - 7$$
$$s = 32$$

$$25 + 32 = 57$$

4. **11 miles:** Let B = the number of miles run by Ben.
Let S = the number of miles run by Sarah.

$$B + S = 30$$
$$B = S - 8$$

$$B + 8 = S$$

$$(B + 8) + B = 30$$
$$2B + 8 = 30$$
$$2B = 22$$
$$B = 11$$

5. **95 donuts:** 13 students ate 3 donuts each: $13 \times 3 = 39$
7 students ate 8 donuts each: $7 \times (8) = 56$

Total = $39 + 56 = 95$

Set 2, Drill 3:

1. **6 slices of pizza:** Let P = the number of slices of pizza eaten by each of the two friends who eat the same amount. Let T = the number of slices of pizza eaten by the third friend.

$$T = P + 2$$

$$P + P + T = 14$$
$$P + P + (P + 2) = 14$$
$$3P + 2 = 14$$
$$3P = 12$$
$$P = 4$$

$$T = P + 2 = 4 + 2 = 6$$

2. **270 miles:** Let F = the distance of the first flight.
Let S = the distance of the second flight.
Let T = the distance of the third flight.

$$F = 2S$$
$$S = 3T$$
$$T = 45$$

$$S = 3 \times (45) = 135$$
$$F = 2 \times (135) = 270$$

3. **30 feet:** Let a = the height of the first bounce.
Let b = the height of the second bounce.

$$a = 5 \times b$$
$$b = 5$$

$$a = 5 \times (5) = 25$$

Total height = $a + b = 25 + 5 = 30$

4. **120 students:** If each tour takes 30 minutes, a guide can complete 4 tours in 2 hours.

4 tours × 30 students = 120 students

5. **300 people:** Let f = the number of people at the first concert.
Let l = the number of people at the last concert.
Let s = the number of people at the sixth concert.

$$f = 100$$
$$l = 6f = 6 \times (100) = 600$$
$$s = 1/2 \, (l) = 1/2 \times (600) = 300$$

Set 2, Drill 4:

1. **$650:** Profit = Revenue − Cost

    Revenue = $300 \times 6 + 300 \times 2 = 1{,}800 + 600 = 2{,}400$

    Cost = 1,750

    Profit = $2{,}400 - 1{,}750 = 650$

2. **290 new members:** Let a = the number of new members recruited by the first company.

    Let b = the number of new members recruited by the second company.

    Let c = the number of new members recruited by the third company.

    $a = 120$

    $b = 2/3\ (a) = 2/3 \times (120) = 80$

    $c = b + 10 = (80) + 10 = 90$

    $a + b + c = 120 + 80 + 90 = 290$

3. **$10,000:** Profit = Revenue − Cost

    Revenue = $50 \times 700 = 35{,}000$

    Cost = $10{,}000 + (50 \times 300) = 10{,}000 + 15{,}000 = 25{,}000$

    Profit = $35{,}000 - 25{,}000 = 10{,}000$

4. **21 hours:** First, let's figure out how many trips we need. If each trip can accommodate 50 people, then we will need:

    350 people/50 = 7 trips

    7 trips $\times$ 3 hours = 21 hours

5. **21 pies:** Let A = the number of pies that Alfred cooked.

    Let N = the number of pies that Nick cooked.

    $A + N = 49$

    $2A = N + 14 \qquad\qquad 2A - 14 = N$

    $A + (2A - 14) = 49$

    $3A - 14 = 49$

    $3A = 63$

    $A = 21$

Set 2, Drill 5:

1. **200 tickets:** Let x = the total number of tickets sold.

    Therefore, $(x - 100)$ = the number of tickets sold over 100.

    $11x + 2(x - 100) = 2{,}400$

    $11x + 2x - 200 = 2{,}400$

    $13x = 2{,}600$

    $x = 200$

2. **1,500 magazines:** Let m = the number of magazines sold.

Total cost = $3m + 10,500$

Total revenue = $10m$

Breaking even occurs when total revenue equals total cost, so:

$3m + 10,500 = 10m$
$10,500 = 7m$
$1,500 = m$

3. **18 games:** Let E = the number of games Eleanor's team won.

Let C = the number of games Christine's team won.

Let J = the number of games Joanna's team won.

$E = 3C$
$C = J - 4$
$J = 10$

$C = (10) - 4 = 6$
$E = 3(6) = 18$

4. **54 miles:** Let $[XY]$ = the distance between Town X and Town Y.

Let $[XZ]$ = the distance between Town X and Town Z.

Let $[ZW]$ = the distance between Town Z and Town W.

Translating the information in the question, we get:

$[XY] = 2[XZ]$	from the first sentence
$[ZW] = 2/3 \, [XZ]$	from the second sentence
$[ZW] = 18$	from the third sentence

$18 = 2/3 \, [XZ]$
$54/2 = [XZ]$
$27 = [XZ]$
$[XY] = 2(27) = 54$

5. **45 hours:** Let h = number of hours Renee worked.

$40(40) + (h - 40)(80) = 2,000$ assuming $h = 40$,
$1,600 + 80h - 3,200 = 2,000$
$80h - 1,600 = 2,000$
$80h = 3,600$
$h = 45$

DRILL SET 3:

Set 3, Drill 1:

1. **18 years old:** Let N = Norman's age now. $(N + 6)$ = Norman's age in 6 years.
Let M = Michael's age now. $(M + 6)$ = Michael's age in 6 years.

$N = M + 12$ Translate the first sentence into an equation.
$N + 6 = 2 (M + 6)$ Translate the second sentence into an equation.

$N - 12 = M$ Rewrite the first equation to put it in terms of M.

$N + 6 = 2(N - 12 + 6)$ Insert $N - 12$ for M in the second equation.
$N + 6 = 2(N - 6)$
$N + 6 = 2N - 12$

$18 = N$ Solve for N.

2. **5 years old:** Let L = Louise's age now. $(L + 5)$ = Louise's age 5 years from now.
Let M = Mary's age now. $(M + 5)$ = Mary's age 5 years from now.

$L = 3M$ Translate the first sentence into an equation.
$(L + 5) = 2(M + 5)$ Translate the second sentence into an equation.

$(3M + 5) = 2(M + 5)$ Insert $3M$ for L in the second equation.
$3M + 5 = 2M + 10$ Make sure you distribute the 2.
$M = 5$ Solve for M

3. **18 years old:** Let C = Chris' age now. $(C + 3)$ = Chris' age 3 years from now.
Let S = Sam's age now. $(S + 3)$ = Sam's age 3 years from now.

$C = S - 14$ Translate the first sentence into an equation.
$3(C + 3) = (S + 3)$ Translate the second sentence into an equation.

$3C + 9 = S + 3$
$3(S - 14) + 9 = S + 3$ Insert $S - 14$ for M in the second equation.
$3S - 42 + 9 = S + 3$
$3S - 33 = S + 3$
$2S - 33 = 3$
$2S = 36$
$S = 18$ Solve for S.

4. **23 years old:** Let T = Toshi's age.
Let K = Kosuke's age.
Let J = Junko's age.

$J = 8$
$B = 2 \times J = 2 \times (8) = 16$
$T = B + 7 = (16) + 7 = 23$

5. **50 years old:** Let A = Amar's age now. $(A + 5)$ = Amar's age 5 years from now.
Let L = Lauri's age now. $(L + 5)$ = Lauri's age 5 years from now.

We're looking for Lauri's age in 10 years: $L + 10$

$A = L - 30$	Translate the first sentence into an equation.
$L + 5 = 3(A + 5)$	Translate the second sentence into an equation.

$L + 5 = 3(L - 30 + 5)$	Insert $L - 30$ for A in the second equation.
$L + 5 = 3(L - 25)$	
$L + 5 = 3L - 75$	
$80 = 2L$	
$40 = L$	

Remember, we're looking for Lauri's age in 10 years:

$L + 10 = 40 + 10 = 50$

Set 3, Drill 2:

1. **$3,600:** Each lawyer worked 4 hours, earning $300 per hour. $4 \times \$300 = \$1,200$

There are 3 lawyers. $\$1,200 \times 3 = \$3,600$

They earned $3,600 in total.

2. **15:** $A = \dfrac{S}{n}$. Here, $10 = A$, S is the sum of the 3 terms $(2, 13, x)$, and 3 is the number of terms.

$$\frac{2 + 13 + x}{3} = 10$$

$$2 + 13 + x = 30$$

$$15 + x = 30$$

$$x = 15$$

3. **$30,000:** Let N = the amount of money Nancy earned.
   Let J = the amount of money Janet earned.
   Let K = the amount of money Kate earned.
   Let A = the average salary.

   $N = 2J$
   $K = 3J$
   $K = \$45,000$

   $(\$45,000) = 3J$
   $\$15,000 = J$

   $N = 2(\$15,000)$
   $N = \$30,000$

   $$\frac{N + K + J}{3} = A$$

   $$\frac{\$30,000 + \$15,000 + \$45,000}{3} = A \quad \frac{\$90,000}{3} = A \quad \$30,000 = A$$

4. **$13:** $\dfrac{\text{Sum}}{\text{Number}} = \text{Average}$.

   First, we need to know the cost of the 5 books.

   Sum = (Average)(Number) = ($12)(5) = $60.

   Sum of the cost of all 6 books = $60 + $18 = $78.
   Number of total books = 6.

   $$\text{Average} = \frac{\$78}{6} = \$13.$$

5. **42:** $\dfrac{(x-3) + (x)(x+3) + (x+4) + (x+11)}{5} = 45$

   $$\frac{5x + 15}{5} = 45$$

   $x + 3 = 45$
   $x = 42$

Set 3, Drill 3:

1. **3 hours:** Let r = rate.
   Let t = time.
   Let d = distance.

   $r \times t = d$
   $(30 \text{ m/hr}) \times t = 90 \text{ miles}$
   $t = 90/30 = 3 \text{ hours}$

2. **2 hours:** Let r = rate.
   Let t = time.
   Let d = distance.
   $r = 4 \text{ miles/hr}$
   $1/2 \times r = 2 \text{ miles/hr}$
   $d = 4 \text{ miles}$

   $r \times t = d$
   $2 \text{ miles/hr} \times t = 4 \text{ miles}$
   $2t = 4$
   $t = 2 \text{ hours}$

3. **70 miles per hour:** $rt = d$
   $r(9 \text{ hours}) = 630 \text{ miles}$
   $r = 70 \text{ miles per hour}$

4. **2 hours:** r = rate at which Randy ran.
   $r + 3$ = the rate at which Betty ran.

   $12 \text{ miles} = r(4 \text{ hours})$
   $r = 3 \text{ miles per hour}$

   $12 = (r + 3)(t)$
   $12 = (3 + 3)(t)$
   $12 = 6t$
   $2 = t$

5. **12 gallons:** Let d = distance traveled

   $d = (60 \text{ mph})(3 \text{ hours}) = 180 \text{ miles}$

   $180 \text{ miles}/15 \text{ miles per gallon} = 12 \text{ gallons}$

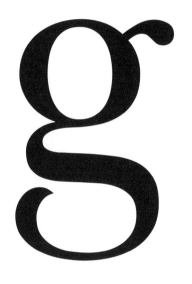

Chapter 10
of
WORD PROBLEMS

WORD PROBLEMS PRACTICE QUESTION SETS

In This Chapter . . .

- Easy Practice Question Set
- Medium Practice Question Set
- Hard Practice Question Set
- Easy Practice Question Solutions
- Medium Practice Question Solutions
- Hard Practice Question Solutions

Word Problems: Easy Practice Question Set

1. Five stand-by passengers are waiting for three open seats on an airplane flight. In how many different ways can three passengers be arranged in these seats?

   (A)   10
   (B)   15
   (C)   20
   (D)   60
   (E) 125

2. When two fair dice are rolled, what is the probability that at least one of the numbers will be even?

   (A) $\dfrac{1}{4}$

   (B) $\dfrac{1}{3}$

   (C) $\dfrac{1}{2}$

   (D) $\dfrac{2}{3}$

   (E) $\dfrac{3}{4}$

3.
                    60% of the students in a classroom are girls.

Quantity A	**Quantity B**
The ratio of boys to girls in the classroom	$\dfrac{3}{5}$

4.
              A pancake recipe calls for $\dfrac{1}{5}$ cup sugar for every cup of flour.

Quantity A	**Quantity B**
Number of cups of sugar in 2 cups of sugar/flour mix	$\dfrac{2}{5}$ cups of sugar

5. A printer can print 12 pages per minute. At that rate, how many <u>seconds</u> will the printer require to print 30 pages?

   (A)   2.5
   (B)   30
   (C)   42
   (D) 150
   (E) 360

6.

Quantity A	**Quantity B**
The average of 34, 46, 42, 30, 38 and 26	36

7. What is the range of the set of odd integers between 4 and 40?

(A) 18
(B) 20
(C) 34
(D) 35
(E) 36

8. Jared drove two hours at an average speed of 50 mph before taking a one hour lunch break. He then drove the remaining 270 miles at an average speed of 60 mph. What was the total time for his trip, in hours?

(A) 2
(B) 4.5
(C) 6.5
(D) 7.5
(E) 9.5

9. At the Golden Buffet, diners can choose between soup or salad for an appetizer; beef, chicken, fish or pasta for an entrée; and pie or ice cream for dessert. What is the maximum number of days that a diner can eat a combination of one appetizer, one entrée and one dessert at the Golden Buffet without repeating the same combination twice?

☐

10. Joe has 5 quarters and 3 nickels. If he picks two of his coins at random, what is the probability that both will be quarters?

(A) $\dfrac{1}{4}$

(B) $\dfrac{5}{14}$

(C) $\dfrac{25}{64}$

(D) $\dfrac{5}{8}$

(E) $\dfrac{2}{3}$

11. A dressing recipe calls for vinegar and oil to be in the ratio 2 : 3 by volume, and for water and oil to be in the ratio 5 : 7 by volume. If there are no other ingredients in the recipe, which of the following statements must be true?

Indicate all such statements.

[A] The dressing will contain more water than vinegar.

[B] At least 25% of the dressing will be vinegar.

[C] There will be 3 ounces of water in 9 ounces of dressing.

[D] If we have equal volumes of each ingredient, the amount of dressing we can mix will be limited by the amount of oil.

12.

At a bakery, donuts cost $0.85 each, and bagels cost $1.10 each.

Quantity A	**Quantity B**
The total cost of a dozen donuts and a dozen bagels at the bakery	$24

13. Two candidates, Steve and Tammy, split the 1,000 votes cast in the election for Student Council President. Which of the following statements, taken individually, are sufficient to determine the number of votes cast for Steve?

Indicate all such statements.

[A] The ratio of Steve's votes to Tammy's votes was 3 : 2.

[B] Tammy received 40% of the votes.

[C] The average of Steve's votes and Tammy's votes was 500.

[D] Steve received 200 more votes than Tammy.

14. A biologist analyzes the number of paramecia visible under a microscope for a collection of protozoa samples. The average number of paramecia visible is 8.1 per sample, and the standard deviation is 2.4. The distribution of paramecia visible across the samples is approximately normally distributed.

Quantity A	**Quantity B**
The number of paramecia visible at the 75th percentile in the distribution of samples	10.5

15. Tom buys oranges and bananas from a local fruit stand. In total he spends $8 and buys 8 pieces of fruit. Bananas are more expensive than oranges.

Quantity A	**Quantity B**
The cost of 2 oranges	$1

16. Andrew brings $5 to the grocery store to buy candy and gum. Candy costs $0.75 apiece and gum costs $1.25 per pack. What's the maximum number of packs of gum Andrew can buy if he buys at least 2 pieces of candy?

   (A) Zero
   (B) One
   (C) Two
   (D) Three
   (E) Four

17.

Jon can finish a race in exactly 4 hours. Stacy runs at a speed that is 50% faster than John's speed.

Quantity A	**Quantity B**
2.5 hours	The amount of time it will take Stacy to complete the race

18.

A bottle of laundry detergent costs $3.60. Each bottle can be used to wash 23 loads of laundry.

Quantity A	**Quantity B**
$40	The approximate cost of the laundry detergent needed to wash 250 loads of laundry

19.

A child must choose from among 5 balloons, each of a different color.

Quantity A	**Quantity B**
The number of combinations of 2 different balloons he can choose	The number of combinations of 3 different balloons he can choose

20. X is the probability that an insurance policy will pay off 100% of the value of a claim, and Y is the probability that an insurance policy will pay off 50% of the value of that claim. No other possible outcomes exist.

Quantity A	**Quantity B**
XY	$X - Y$

Word Problems: Medium Practice Question Set

1. Joe will pick 3 friends to join him on a road trip. Among his friends are 4 musicians and 3 poets. In how many different ways can Joe select his 3 traveling companions so that he has at least one musician and at least one poet among them?

    (A) 16
    (B) 18
    (C) 30
    (D) 36
    (E) 84

2. A car gets 18 miles per gallon of gasoline in city driving and 24 miles per gallon on the highway. Gasoline costs $3 per gallon.

Quantity A	**Quantity B**
The minimum possible fuel cost of driving 420 miles	$50

3. The five offensive linemen on a football team weigh 295, 310, 304, 321 and 298 pounds, respectively. When the heaviest lineman is injured and replaced by a teammate, the average weight of the five linemen drops by 2 pounds. What is the range of the weights of the new group of five linemen?

    (A) 10
    (B) 15
    (C) 16
    (D) 24
    (E) 26

4. Towns X and Y are 220 miles apart along a road. Car A, traveling at 20 miles per hour, leaves from Town X towards Town Y at the same time as Car B, traveling at 35 miles per hour, leaves Town Y towards Town X. How many miles will Car B have traveled when the two cars pass by each other?

    (A) 55
    (B) 70
    (C) 80
    (D) 110
    (E) 140

5. The average weight of the men in a meeting room is 170 pounds, and the average weight of the women is 130 pounds. If more than 60% of the people in the room are men, which of the following could be the average weight of all people in the room?

   Select <u>all</u> choices that apply:

   A 144
   B 148
   C 150
   D 152
   E 154
   F 156
   G 158
   H 168

6.

Score	64	70	72	79	83	85	90	94	95
Number of students achieving that score	1	2	1	4	4	2	3	2	1

The frequency distribution of student scores on a test is as shown above. How many of the scores are above the class average?

7. Two journalists have 8 hours in which to copy-edit a total of 100 articles. If Journalist A copy-edits at a steady rate of 3.5 articles per hour, how many articles per hour must Journalist B copy-edit in order to complete the assignment on time?

   (A) 12.5
   (B) 9
   (C) 8
   (D) 4.5
   (E) 3

8. The ratio of violinists to cellists at a conservatory is 3 to 1. 180 of the violinists depart, and all the cellists remain, resulting in a new ratio of 3 violinists to 2 cellists. How many cellists are enrolled at the conservatory?

9. The ratio of boys to girls in a certain coed school is greater than 1. When 2 boys leave and 3 girls are added to the school, the ratio still favors boys. What is the least number of boys that could have been originally enrolled in the school, assuming there was originally <u>at least</u> one girl?

   (A)   1
   (B)   4
   (C)   5
   (D)   7
   (E) 13

10.

Asset	Amount Invested	Expected Return
Stock X	$40	10%
Stock Y	$40	8%
Stock Z	$20	15%

<u>Quantity A</u>   <u>Quantity B</u>

The percent return an investor would expect for   10.5%
investing the amounts listed in the above stocks

11. Roger bought some pencils and erasers at the stationery store. If he bought more pencils than erasers, and the total number of the pencils and erasers he bought is between 12 and 20 (inclusive), which of the following statements must be true?

   Select <u>all</u> that apply.

   A Roger bought no fewer than 7 pencils.
   B Roger bought no more than 12 pencils.
   C Roger bought no fewer than 6 erasers.
   D Roger bought no more than 9 erasers.

12. 40% of the attendees at an event are over 50 years old, and another 20% are under 20 years old. Which of the following statements must be true?

   Indicate <u>all</u> such statements.

   A The ratio of those over 50 to those between 20 and 50 is 2: 3.
   B The ratio of those under 20 to those between 20 and 50 is 1: 2.
   C $\frac{1}{3}$ of the attendees who are not over 50 are under 20.
   D There are at least 10 attendees.

13.

Five years ago, Abigail was half as old as Ben. Next year the sum of their ages will be 27.

Quantity A	**Quantity B**
Abigail's age next year	Ben's age 5 years ago

14. The average weight of a set X of 100 bags of rice is 90 pounds, and the standard deviation of the weights is 8 pounds. Bag A weighs 2 standard deviations below the average weight of the bags in set X. Bag B weighs 5 pounds more than the average.

Quantity A	**Quantity B**
Twice the difference between the weight of Bag B and the weight of Bag A	The range of weights of the bags of rice in set X

15. The probability of rainfall in City X on any given day is 30%. The probability of rainfall on any given day is independent of whether it rains on any other day.

Quantity A	**Quantity B**
The probability of rainfall in City X on <u>at least</u> one day out of two days	The probability of no rainfall in City X on either of those two days

16. State Y charges a 4% tax on all residential household telephone lines each month, rounded to the nearest penny. Customer A spends less than $50 each month on his telephone bill, including tax.

Quantity A	**Quantity B**
$48	The cost of Customer A's telephone bill _before_ tax

17. Jennifer can purchase 11-cent and 21-cent stamps. If she intends to spend <u>exactly</u> $2.84 on these stamps, which of the following is a possible number of 11-cent stamps she can purchase?

(A) Zero
(B) One
(C) Two
(D) Three
(E) Four

18.

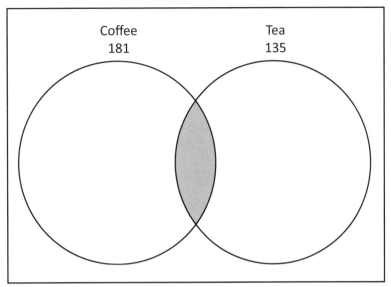

Total Consumers Polled: 305

Coffee
181

Tea
135

In a sample of 305 consumers polled, 181 drink coffee, and 135 drink tea. The grey area in the diagram represents the consumers who drink both.

Quantity A	**Quantity A**
The number of consumers polled who consume _both_ coffee and tea	The number of consumers polled who consume _neither_ coffee nor tea

19. In a recreation club with 212 members, 130 participate in kickboxing, and 110 participate in rowing. If at least 10% of the club's members participate in neither kickboxing nor rowing, what's the minimum number of members who participate in both?

20. A pomegranate grower packages pomegranates in 10-pound and 20-pound boxes. If the grower fills more than twice as many 20-pound boxes as 10-pound boxes, which of the following could be the percentage of pomegranates, by weight, that are packaged in 10-pound boxes?

(A) 15%
(B) 20%
(C) 25%
(D) 40%
(E) 60%

Word Problems: Hard Practice Question Set

CAUTION: These problems are *very difficult*—more difficult than many of the problems you will likely see on the GRE. Conside these "Challenge Problems." Have fun!

1. A steel bar 135 inches long will be cut into a number of five inch and seven inch segments, with no part of the original steel bar left over.

Quantity A	**Quantity B**
The minimum possible number of five inch pieces	5

2. A drawer contains 6 brown socks and 4 black socks. What is the probability that the first two socks pulled from the drawer will be of the same color?

(A) $\dfrac{1}{3}$

(B) $\dfrac{7}{15}$

(C) $\dfrac{1}{2}$

(D) $\dfrac{8}{15}$

(E) $\dfrac{2}{3}$

3.

Four people each roll a fair die once.

Quantity A	**Quantity B**
The probability that *at least* two people will roll the same number	70%

4. A company employs 20 workers for every 3 managers, and 5 managers for every director. If the total number of employees at the company is between 300 and 400, the number of managers who work at the company must equal what?

[   ]

5. A set of integers consists of 2, 3, 5, 7, 11, 12 and *x*. If *x* increases by 1, the median of the set stays unchanged. However, if *x* decreases by 1, the median of the set also decreases by 1. What is the value of *x*?

[   ]

6. Jane can flip 40 pancakes per minute, while Sally works at half Jane's rate. How many minutes will it take the two of them to flip 150 pancakes, if Sally flips the first 30 by herself and is then joined by Jane for the remainder?

   Express your answer in decimal notation: [   ]

7. Jake rides his bike for the first $\frac{2}{3}$ of the distance from home to school, traveling at 10 miles per hour. He

   then walks the remaining $\frac{1}{3}$ of the distance at 3 miles per hour. If his total trip takes 40 minutes, how many

   miles is it from Jake's home to his school?

   (A) $\frac{5}{4}$

   (B) $\frac{15}{4}$

   (C) 5
   (D) 6
   (E) 10

8. John is to select a committee of 4 individuals from among a group of 5 candidates. The committee will have a President, a Vice President and two Treasurers. How many different committees can John select from the 5 candidates?

   [   ]

9. John is organizing a charity event in an effort to raise money to build a neighborhood park. The park will cost $1,200 to build. Each person attending the event will donate $300, less $20 for each person who attends the event. Thus, for example, if 3 people attend the event, each person will donate $300 − $20(3) = $240. What is the minimum number of people who must attend the event in order to raise enough money to build the park?

   (A) 4
   (B) 5
   (C) 6
   (D) 8
   (E) John cannot raise enough money at this charity event to build the park.

10. Country X has three coins in its currency: a *duom* worth 2 cents, a *trippim* worth 11 cents, and a *megam* worth 19 cents. If a man has $3.21 worth of Country X's currency and cannot carry more than 20 coins, what is the least number of *trippim* he could have?

    (A) 0
    (B) 1
    (C) 2
    (D) 3
    (E) It cannot be determined.

11. In a certain class, $\frac{1}{5}$ of the boys are shorter than the shortest girl in the class and $\frac{1}{3}$ of the girls are taller than the tallest boy in the class. If there are 16 students in the class and no two people have the same height, what percent of the students are taller than the shortest girl and shorter than the tallest boy?

(A)   25%
(B)   50%
(C) 62.5%
(D) 66.7%
(E)   75%

12. What is the range of the set $\left\{ \frac{2}{3}, \frac{8}{11}, \frac{5}{8}, \frac{4}{7}, \frac{9}{13} \right\}$?

Express the result as a fraction: $\dfrac{\boxed{}}{\boxed{}}$

13. The value of 30 oobers equals the value of 12 darbles, and the value of 5 muxes equals the value of 20 oobers. What is the ratio of the value of two muxes to that of one darble?

Express the result as a fraction: $\dfrac{\boxed{}}{\boxed{}}$

14. In a race, at least three and at most five runners will vie for gold, silver and bronze medals. Which of the following could represent the total number of unique ways to distribute the three medals among the participants?

Indicate all such numbers.

[A]   3
[B]   6
[C] 12
[D] 24
[E] 30
[F] 60

15. Carla has $\frac{1}{4}$ more sweaters than cardigans, and $\frac{2}{5}$ fewer cardigans than turtlenecks. If she has at least one of each item, what is the minimum total number of <u>turtlenecks plus sweaters</u> that Carla could have?

$\boxed{}$

16. In a class of 500 students, an examination was given. Scores were given on an integer scale of 0-100. Joe scored 2 standard deviations above the mean score on the examination, and Charlie's score was at exactly the 5th percentile. The distribution of exam scores was approximately normal. Which of the following statements *must* be true?

Indicate <u>all</u> such statements:

   [A] Joe scored closer to the mean than Charlie.

   [B] More than 400 students achieved scores lower than or equal to Joe's score and higher than or equal to Charlie's score.

   [C] Fewer than 450 students achieved scores lower than or equal to Joe's score and higher than or equal to Charlie's score.

   [D] At least one other person received the same score as Charlie.

17. The probability of Tom rolling a strike while bowling is 40% on any given frame. If Tom rolls 4 frames in a row, which of the following statements are true?

Indicate <u>all</u> such statements.

   [A] The probability of Tom rolling a strike on all 4 frames is greater than 3%.

   [B] The probability of Tom rolling no strikes in 4 frames is less than 10%.

   [C] Tom is equally likely to roll exactly 1 strike as to roll exactly 2 strikes in those 4 frames.

   [D] Tom will roll 2 or more strikes less than half the time.

18. It takes h minutes to fill a hot tub with a hot water hose and c minutes to fill it with a cold-water hose, where c is smaller than h.

Quantity A	**Quantity B**
$\dfrac{h^2}{c+h}$	The number of minutes required to fill the hot tub using the hot water hose and the cold water hose simultaneously

19. 1,500 individuals attended a marathon held in Town A. Of those, only y participated in the marathon. If x of the 1,500 individuals were from Town A, and z of the individiuals participated in the marathon but were not from Town A, which of the following represents the number of individuals who did not participate in the marathon and were not from Town A?

   (A) $1,500 - x + 2y$
   (B) $1,500 - x + 2z$
   (C) $1,500 - x - y + z$
   (D) $1,500 - x + y - z$
   (A) $1,500 - x - z$

20. How many 3-digit integers can be chosen such that none of the digits appear more than twice, and none of the digits equal zero?

   (A) 729
   (B) 720
   (C) 648
   (D) 640
   (E) 576

Word Problems: Easy Practice Question Solutions

1. **D:** This is a typical Permutation problem, in which _order matters_ and three people are to be chosen from a pool of five. The total number of possible selections is given by the formula $\dfrac{\text{Pool!}}{\text{Out!}}$, where "Out" is the number of items (people) _not_ to be chosen. This yields $\dfrac{5!}{2!} = 5 \times 4 \times 3 = 60$.

We can also solve this problem by using the Anagram Method. Five people (call them A through E) will be assigned to seats (designated as _1_, _2_, and _3_), with two people left without a seat (designated as _N_):

A	B	C	D	E
_1_	_2_	_3_	_N_	_N_

The total number of possibilities is the number of arrangements of the "word" _123NN_, which yields the same formula as above: 5 items, so 5!, divided by a factorial for all "repeats." The _N_ is listed twice, so the correct expression is $\dfrac{5!}{2!}$.

2. **E:** Problems of this type (characterized by wording such as "at least") are often most easily solved using the "$1 - x$" Shortcut. It is easier to solve for the probability of the event _not_ happening, because it is easily defined: both numbers come up odd.

The probability of each number coming up odd is $\dfrac{3}{6} = \dfrac{1}{2}$. Since the two dice are independent, the probability of

both coming up odd is $\dfrac{1}{2} \times \dfrac{1}{2} = \dfrac{1}{4}$, so the probability of getting at least one even number is $1 - \dfrac{1}{4} = \dfrac{3}{4}$.

3. **A:** If 60% of the students are girls, then 40% must be boys. Thus, the ratio of boys to girls is $\dfrac{40}{60} = \dfrac{2}{3}$, which is

about 67% (and thus greater than $\dfrac{3}{5}$, which equals 60%). Alternatively, we can compare $\dfrac{2}{3}$ to $\dfrac{3}{5}$ by cross-multiply-

ing and comparing the numerators: $\dfrac{2}{3}$ is to $\dfrac{3}{5}$ as 10 is to 9. **Quantity A is greater.**

4. **B:** The ratio of sugar to flour is $\dfrac{1}{5}$ to 1, or 1 to 5. Therefore the ratio of sugar to flour to _combined mix_ is 1:5:6.

We can now use a Proportion to determine the number of cups of sugar: 1 cup of sugar is to 6 cups of mix, as x cups

of sugar are to 2 cups of mix: $\dfrac{1}{6} = \dfrac{x}{2}$, so $6x = 2$ and $x = \dfrac{1}{3}$. The comparison now becomes:

$$\dfrac{1}{3} \qquad\qquad\qquad\qquad \dfrac{2}{5}$$

Thus **Quantity B is greater.**

5. **D:** The printer's rate of work is $R = 12$ pages/minute, and the total amount of work is $W = 30$ pages. Using the Work Equation $R \times t = W$, we can solve for the time as $t = \dfrac{W}{R} = \dfrac{30}{12} = 2\dfrac{1}{2}$ minutes. However, the question asks for the answer in _seconds_. Because there are 60 seconds in each minute, we must multiply 2.5×60 to arrive at the correct answer of 150 seconds.

6. **C:** When the numbers given in Quantity A are written in ascending order, it can be seen that they are evenly spaced in increments of 4: the set becomes {26, 30, 34, 38, 42, 46}. The average (mean) of an evenly spaced set is the same as its median, which is the middle number. In this case, because the number of terms is even, the median is given by the average of the middle two terms: $\dfrac{34 + 38}{2} = 36$. **The two quantities are equal.**

7. **C:** The odd integers in the interval 4 to 40 run from 5 to 39, inclusive. The range of a set is found by subtracting its smallest member from the largest member: $39 - 5 = 34$.

8. **D:** This problem requires the application of the rate formula, $R \times t = D$. For the second part of his drive,

$t = \dfrac{D}{R} = \dfrac{270}{60} = 4.5$ hours. He also drove two hours before lunch and had a 1 hour lunch break. Thus, the total time

for his trip was $4.5 + 2 + 1 = 7.5$ hours.

9. **16:** The choices of appetizer, entrée and dessert are independent of each other. Independent choices multiply. Because there are 2 options for the appetizer, 4 options for the entrée and 2 options for the dessert, the total number of unique combinations is $2 \times 4 \times 2 = 16$.

10. **B:** We can approach this problem as a "choosing without replacement" problem. First Joe will pick one of 8 coins, 5 of which are quarters. The probability of his picking a quarter is therefore $\dfrac{5}{8}$. Let us suppose that this indeed happens in his first draw. Then, there will be 7 coins left to choose from, and 4 of them will be quarters. (This is the Domino Effect.) The likelihood of picking a quarter next is now $\dfrac{4}{7}$.

The probability of Joe picking quarters _both_ times is found by multiplying the individual probabilities of the two successive events: $P = \dfrac{5}{8} \times \dfrac{4}{7} = \dfrac{5}{14}$.

11. **A, B, and D:** We can write the given relationships as $V : O = 2 : 3$ and $W : O = 5 : 7$. In order to combine both expressions into a single overall ratio, we first need to make sure that the common element in the two ratios (namely oil) appears as the same number in both ratios. The least common multiple of 3 and 7 is 21, so if we multiply the first ratio by 7 and the second ratio by 3, we can achieve our goal: $V : O = 14 : 21$ and $W : O = 15 : 21$, such that $V : O : W : \text{Total} = 14 : 21 : 15 : 50$ (note that the 50 in the combined ratio is simply the sum of the preceding numbers.)

We can now see that Choice A is true: water to vinegar is in the ratio 15:14. Choice B is also correct: vinegar makes up $\dfrac{14}{50} = 28\%$ of the mixture.

Choice C is false, because $\dfrac{15}{50} = \dfrac{3}{10}$ or 30%, not $\dfrac{3}{9}$ or $\dfrac{1}{3}$.

Finally, Choice D is also correct because we can see that the item we consume the most of is oil. Therefore, given equal amounts to begin with, we will run out of oil the soonest.

12. **B:** One option is to calculate the cost of a dozen donuts and a dozen bagels and add them together. The former is $0.85 × 12 = $10.20 and the latter is $1.10 × 12 = $13.20, so that the total cost is $10.20 + $13.20 = $23.20. This is best done using the Calculator.

However, there is an easier approach that requires no heavy calculation: consider that the total cost of one donut and one bagel is $0.85 + $1.10 = $1.95. This is less than $2. Therefore, the total cost of a dozen each of donuts and bagels must be <u>less than</u> $2 × 12 = $24. **Quantity B is greater.**

13. **A, B, and D:** Let S stand for the number of votes cast for Steve. Because the total number of votes was 1,000, the number of votes cast for Tammy must equal $1,000 - S$. (Note that we could have defined a second variable T to stand for Tammy's votes, but it is good practice in general to reduce the number of unknowns. Since the problem asks us to determine the number of votes cast for Steve, we have chosen S as the primary variable and expressed Tammy's votes in terms of S.)

Choice A states that $\dfrac{S}{1,000 - S} = \dfrac{3}{2}$. S can be solved by cross-multiplying. This is a correct answer.

Choice B allows us to solve for S by observing that $1,000 - S = \dfrac{40}{100} \times 1,000 = 400$. This is a correct answer.

Choice C tells us nothing new, because the number of total votes is fixed at 1,000. Therefore, the average of Steve's votes and Tammy's votes, which is the sum of their votes divided by two, *has* to equal 500. This is an incorrect answer.

Finally, Choice D tells us that $S - (1,000 - S) = 200$, which is an equation that we use to solve for S. This is a correct answer.

14. **B:** The 75th percentile of an approximately normally distributed variable is just shy of 1 standard deviation higher than the mean. (About $\dfrac{2}{3}$ of all observations fall within one standard deviation of the mean, so one standard deviation above the mean lives at approximately the $50\text{th} + (100) \times \left(\dfrac{1}{2}\right)\left(\dfrac{2}{3}\right) \approx 83\text{rd}$ percentile.)

Quantity B is $10.5 - 8.1 = 2.4$ units above the mean, or exactly 1 standard deviation above the mean. Therefore,

Quantity B is greater.

15. **D:** If $8 purchases 8 pieces of fruit, and bananas are more expensive than oranges, then the cost of a banana is greater than $1 and the cost of an orange is less than $1. However, this is not sufficient information to answer the question. For example, it's possible that Tom bought 6 bananas at $1.20 apiece ($7.20 total), and 2 oranges at $0.40 apiece ($0.80 total). Alternatively, it's possible that Tom bought 6 bananas at $1.10 apiece ($6.60 total), and 2 oranges at $0.70 apiece ($1.40 total). **We cannot determine** whether 2 oranges cost more or less than $1.

16. **C:** If Andrew purchases 2 pieces of candy, he will have $5 - 2 × $0.75 = $3.50 remaining.

$\dfrac{\$3.50}{\$1.25} = \dfrac{350}{125} = \dfrac{70}{25} = \dfrac{14}{5} = 2.8$ packs of gum is then all he can afford to purchase. Since a fraction/decimal number of packs of gum is impossible to buy, Andrew can only buy 2 packs of gum.

17. **B:** We can use the Distance Formula to help solve this problem: $D = R \times t$. For John, we can divide by R to get $t = \dfrac{D}{R} = 4$. Furthermore, we know that Stacy runs 50% faster than John, So $R_S = (1 + 0.5) \times R = 1.5R$. Plugging this into the equation, we get: $t_S = \dfrac{D}{R_S} = \dfrac{D}{1.5R} = 4\left(\dfrac{1}{1.5}\right) = \dfrac{4}{1.5} = \dfrac{8}{3}$ hours. This is slightly larger than Quantity A, 2.5 hours, so **Quantity B is larger.**

18. **A:** If a \$3.60 bottle of laundry detergent can be used to wash 23 loads, then the cost per load is $\dfrac{\$3.60}{23} \approx \$0.1565$ per load of laundry. Therefore the cost of 250 loads of laundry is approximately $250 \times \$0.1565 = \$39.13$.

Thus **Quantity A is larger** by about \$0.87.

This calculation can be made almost precisely by making use of the Calculator.

19. **C:** The number of ways that a child can choose a set of 2 balloons out of 5 is given by (5 Choose 2): $\dfrac{5!}{3! \times 2!} = 10$ different possible sets. Similarly, the number of ways that a child can choose a set of 3 balloons out of 5 is given by (5 Choose 3): $\dfrac{5!}{2! \times 3!} = 10$ different possible sets. Thus **the two quantities are equal.**

At first the fact that these two quantities are equal may seem surprising. However upon further inspection, we can see that choosing 2 balloons out of 5 is the same as choosing 3 balloons out of 5: when we choose 2 items out of 5, we are simultaneously choosing to <u>exclude</u> 3 items from our choice. We are effectively dividing the 5 balloons into a "Yes" pool and a "No" pool. The second scenario is the reverse of this: we are saying "Yes" to 3 balloons and "No" to 2 balloons. There are the <u>same number of ways</u> to say "Yes" to 2 balloons out of 5 as there are to say "No" to 2 balloons out of 5.

20. **D:** The only constraints given in the problem are that the probabilities X and Y must sum to 1, because no other possible outcomes exist. However, nothing more is known about the relative size of X and Y. For example, if $X = 0.4$, then $Y = 0.6$ and XY is positive while $X - Y$ is negative. By contrast, if $X = 0.8$, then $Y = 0.2$, $XY = 0.16$ and $X - Y = 0.6$. Therefore, either quantity could be larger. **We do not have enough information** to answer the question.

Word Problems: Medium Practice Question Solutions

1. **C:** Joe has to select either two musicians and one poet, or one musician and two poets. The number of ways he can select two musicians from among 4 is given by $\frac{4!}{2! \times 2!} = \frac{24}{4} = 6$, while the number of ways to select one poet from among 3 is 3. Thus, there are $6 \times 3 = 18$ ways to select two musicians and one poet. Similarly, the number of ways to select one musician from among 4 is 4, while the number of ways to select two poets out of 3 is $\frac{3!}{2! \times 1!} = \frac{6}{2} = 3$. This gives Joe another $4 \times 3 = 12$ ways to select his traveling companions. The total number of options Joe has is

$18 + 12 = 30$.

2. **A:** In order to incur the least possible cost in fuel, the car must be driven on the highway for the entire 420 miles, so that the higher mile per gallon figure applies. The number of gallons of fuel required for the trip is given by $\frac{420}{24} = \frac{35}{2} = 17\frac{1}{2}$ gallons. The cost of the fuel is \$3 times this minimum number of gallons:

The minimum possible fuel cost of driving 420 miles =

$$\$3 \times 17\frac{1}{2} = \mathbf{\$52\frac{1}{2}} \qquad\qquad\qquad \mathbf{\$50}$$

Therefore **Quantity A is greater.**

3. **C:** If the replacement of one player by another lowers the average weight by 2 pounds, we can conclude that the sum of the five weights must have dropped by $2 \times 5 = 10$. This is because the average equals the sum divided by the number of terms.

Based on the 10 pound drop in total weight, we can further conclude that the heaviest lineman, who weighed 321 pounds, must have been replaced by a teammate who weighs 311 pounds and is now the heaviest of the group. The range of weights is found by subtracting the weight of the lightest lineman (295 pounds) from 311. $311 - 295 = 16$.

4. **E:** One way to solve this problem is to use an *RTD* chart, as shown below:

Car	R (miles/hour)	T (hours)	D (miles)
A	20	t	20t
B	35	t	35t

The times for the two cars are equal, because they start simultaneously. The sum of the distances traveled by the two cars must equal 220 miles. We can solve for t from $20t + 35t = 55t = 220$, yielding $t = 4$ hours. The distance traveled by Car B is then found as follows: $R \times t = 35 \times 4 = 140$ miles.

An alternative method would be to add the rates of the two cars, since they are traveling towards each other. The combined rate of 55 miles per hour is the rate at which the initial distance of 220 miles shrinks to zero. This will also lead us to $t = 4$ hours.

Yet another approach is to tabulate the distances traveled by the two cars every hour, continuing until the total distance equals 220 miles.

5. F, G, and **H:** This problem can be solved as a Weighted Average problem. The overall average weight will be between 130 and 170 pounds, but closer to 170 pounds because there are more men than women in the room. We can use the limiting percentage of 60 to establish the lower bound on the overall average weight: if the percentage of men is greater than 60, then the result will be higher than this lower bound. The "weights" to use in the Weighted Average formula are 60% or $\frac{3}{5}$ for the men and 40% or $\frac{2}{5}$ for the women. The lower bound on the average weight is thus: $\frac{3}{5} \times 170 + \frac{2}{5} \times 130 = 102 + 52 = 154$ pounds. This value is _not_ possible, because the percentage of men is greater than 60; however all the values _higher than_ 154 are possible.

6. 12: The total number of student test scores is found by adding the numbers in the second row; the result is 20. We can find the average score by dividing the sum of all scores by 20. The sum of all scores is best found using the memory function of the Calculator. First, make sure that the memory is clear by pressing MC. Then, multiply each score by its frequency and add the result to the running sum in memory: $64 \times 1 = M+$, $70 \times 2 = M+$, etc., up to $95 \times 1 = M+$. At that point, retrieve the sum from memory using MR (the result is 1,647) and divide by 20 to obtain 82.35 as the average score. Finally, from the table, add up the number of students who scored 83 and above to obtain the final answer of 12.

7. B: In order to find Journalist A's work, we must multiply rate × time: $R \times t = W$. 3.5 articles per hour × 8 hours = 28 articles. Journalist B must therefore copy-edit $100 - 28 = 72$ articles.

To find Journalist B's rate, we simply plug 72 for Work into the work formula and solve for B's rate. $R_B \times 8$ hours = 72, so $R_B = 9$ articles per hour.

Alternately, since the journalists are working on the same task over the same time interval, we can combine their rates:

$$(R_A + R_B) \times 8 \text{ hours} = 100$$
$$(R_A + R_B) = 12.5$$
$$(3.5 + R_B) = 12.5$$
$$R_B = 9$$

8. 120: The original ratio can be expressed in a proportion equation:

$$\frac{v}{c} = \frac{3}{1}$$
$$v = 3c$$

After the departure of 180 violinists, we have a new proportion:

$$\frac{v - 180}{c} = \frac{3}{2}$$

We now have two equations and two variables and can combine and solve. Since we are solving for c, we should simplify and substitute for v first:

$$\frac{v-180}{c} = \frac{3}{2}$$
$$2(v-180) = 3c$$
$$2v - 360 = 3c$$
$$2(3c) - 360 = 3c$$
$$3c = 360$$
$$c = 120$$

Therefore there are 120 cellists.

We might also notice that when the 180 violinists depart, the ratio of violinists to cellists is cut in half. Therefore, 180 must have been half of the violinists. Originally, then, there must have been 360 violinists. Since there were 3 times as many violinists as cellists, there were $\frac{360}{3} = 120$ cellists.

9. **D**: Because the ratio of boys to girls is greater than 1, we know that there are more boys than girls in this school:

$$b > g$$

When two boys leave and three girls are added the ratio is still greater than one, so we can say: $\frac{b-2}{g+3} > 1$.

Solving:

$$b - 2 > g + 3$$
$$b > g + 5$$

Because we want to minimize b, we choose g to be as small as possible. The school is coed and the boy/girl ratio is greater than 1, so the smallest number of girl students is 1. Thus we choose $g = 1$ to yield $b > 6$. Therefore, the least number of boys that could have been originally enrolled in the school is 7. Checking, we note that with 7 boys and 1 girl originally enrolled in the school, and when 2 boys leave and 3 girls are added, the new ratio is $\frac{5}{4}$, which is greater than 1.

10. **B**: The investor invests $100 total. The weighted averages formula states that the expected return would be equal to (percent invested in X)(expected return of X) + (percent invested in Y)(expected return of Y) + (percent invested in Z)(expected return of Z). Hence the expected return would be: (40%)(10%) + (40%)(8%) + (20%)(15%) = (4%) + (3.2%) + (3%) = 10.2%.

If you choose to use the calculator, you would enter (0.4 × 10) + (0.4 × 8) + (0.2 × 15) to yield 10.2. To store the products along the way, use the M+ or MR keys.

10.2%   10.5%

Therefore **Quantity B is greater.**

11. **A** and **D:** Choice A is true because Roger would have bought at least 7 pencils (to go with 5 erasers) if he bought the minimum possible total number of items. (6 of each is impossible. By the same example, Choice C is disproved.) If he bought more than 12 items, the number of pencils could not be any less than 7 and still be greater than the number of erasers.

On the other hand, Choice B need not be true, because Roger could have bought as many as 19 pencils, even if we assume that he has to buy at least one of each item.

Finally, Choice D must be true, because even if Roger bought the maximum possible number of items (20), less than half of those would have to be erasers. Thus 9 erasers is the most he could have purchased. 10 of each is impossible.

12. **B** and **C:** We can see that $100\% - 40\% - 20\% = 40\%$ of the attendees are between 20 and 50 years old. Thus Choice A is untrue; the real ratio is $40: 40 = 1: 1$. On the other hand, Choice B is true, because $20: 40 = 1: 2$. Choice C is also true, because 60% of the attendees are <u>not</u> over 50, and of those, 20% (or $\frac{1}{3}$ of 60%) are under 20.

Choice D requires a little more thinking. There is a Hidden Constraint in the problem because the number of attendees must be an integer. Expressed as fractions, the percentages of those over 50, between 20 and 50, and under 20 are $\frac{2}{5}, \frac{2}{5}$, and $\frac{1}{5}$, respectively. This means that the total number of attendees has to be divisible by 5. The smallest such number is 5. Thus, Choice D is not necessarily true.

13. **A:** Age problems such as this are best solved by way of a table. Generally it is best to include "now" as one of the times of interest, even if (as in this case) there is no data that specifically refers to the ages today. This is because accounting for times other than now becomes more straightforward when variables are defined to represent the ages today. Based on the problem, we assign A to be Abigail's age now. Then, we can fill in the top row of our table as shown:

Person	Age 5 years ago	Age now	Age next year
Abigail	$A - 5$	A	$A + 1$
Ben			

Next, we can use the relationship that Abigail was half as old as Ben five years ago, to express Ben's age five years ago:

Person	Age 5 years ago	Age now	Age next year
Abigail	$A - 5$	A	$A + 1$
Ben	$2(A - 5) = 2A - 10$		

We can now propagate Ben's age across the years by adding 5 years, and then 1 more year:

Person	Age 5 years ago	Age now	Age next year
Abigail	$A - 5$	A	$A + 1$
Ben	$2A - 10$	$(2A - 10) + 5 = 2A - 5$	$(2A - 5) + 1 = 2A - 4$

The final step is to set the sum of the ages next year equal to 27. This gives $(A + 1) + (2A - 4) = 3A - 3 = 27$, such that $3A = 30$ and $A = 10$. The table now reads as follows:

Person	Age 5 years ago	Age now	Age next year
Abigail	5	10	11
Ben	10	15	16

Since Abigail next year will be one year older than Ben was 5 years ago, **Quantity A is greater.**

14. **D:** The information in the problem relates the weights of Bag A and Bag B to the average weight of the bags in the sample. Since Bag A is 2 standard deviations below normal weight, its weight is $90 - 2 \times 8 = 74$ pounds, and the difference between the weight of Bag B versus that of Bag A is $(90 + 5) - 74 = 95 - 74 = 21$. Thus twice that difference is 42.

The range of the weight of the bags in set X could be less than, more than, or equal to 42. Dividing by the standard deviation, this implies a range equivalent to $\frac{42}{8} = 5.25$ standard deviations, which would be a large standardized range for a sample, but it's possible that the actual range is larger than that. **We do not have enough information** to answer the question.

15. **A:** The probability of rainfall on at least one of the two days is equal to P(Rain 1st day) + P(Rain 2nd day) − P(Rain both days), since rainfall on each day is independent of what happened on other days. This probability equals $0.3 + 0.3 - (0.3 \times 0.3) = 0.6 - 0.09 = 0.51$ or 51%.

Alternatively, we can use the "$1 - x$" trick here: the probability of rainfall on at least one of the two days is 1 − the probability of rain on neither day (0.7^2). Therefore the probability is $1 - 0.7 \times 0.7 = 1 - 0.49 = 0.51 = 51\%$.

Quantity B, the probability of no rainfall on either day, follows from the work above: $0.7 \times 0.7 = 0.49$ or 49%.

Thus **Quantity A is greater.**

16. **D:** The total value of the bill is equal to the original value of the bill, plus 4% of that original value. To use algebra, $T = O + 0.04O = 1.04O$, where O is the original value of the bill (pre-taxes) and T is the total cost of the bill (including taxes).

The question states that for Customer A, $T < 50$. Therefore $1.04O < 50$, and $O < \frac{\$50}{1.04} \approx \$48.07$. Therefore the original bill could have cost $48.07 (tax of $1.92), or $48 (tax of $1.92), or $30 (tax of $1.20). **We do not have**

enough information to answer the question.

17. **B:** 11 and 21 are relatively prime numbers (meaning, they do not share any prime factors in common). Therefore, it is more likely that only a few possible combinations of 11-cent and 21-cent stamps will add up to exactly $2.84. The easiest way to test this is to try each of the Choices, and see whether the remaining money (after buying the given number of 11-cent stamps) results in exactly the right amount of money to buy some integer number of 21-cent stamps:

Number of 11-cent stamps	Cash remaining after purchasing 11-cent stamps	Number of 21-cent stamps (nearest hundredth)
0	$2.84	13.52 (INCORRECT)
1	**$2.73**	**13 (CORRECT)**
2	$2.62	12.48 (INCORRECT)
3	$2.51	11.95 (INCORRECT)
4	$2.40	11.43 (INCORRECT)

It can be shown, incidentally, that the only other combination which works is to purchase 22 11-cent stamps ($2.42) and 2 21-cent stamps ($0.42).

18. **A:** The number of coffee drinkers plus the number of tea drinkers is equal to $181 + 135 = 316$. Because there are only a total of 305 consumers who were surveyed, at least $316 - 305 = 11$ consumers must consume both (assuming that none of those polled failed to drink at least one of the beverages). Thus in this case, there were 11 more consumers of both beverages than of neither beverage. To take the other extreme, assume all 135 tea drinkers also drink coffee. Then $305 - 181 = 124$ consumers would drink neither of the beverages—versus 135 who drank both. Once again, the "both" category exceeds the "neither" category by 11.

It can be shown that this difference of 11 will be constant <u>irrespective</u> of how many consumers fall into the "both" category. **Quantity A will always be 11 larger** than Quantity B.

19. **50:** At least 10% of the recreation club participates in neither kickboxing nor rowing. Therefore at least $10\%(212) = 21.2$ people are in neither activity. Since only integer numbers of members can exist, at least 22 members must not participate in either activity. We can draw a Venn Diagram to illustrate this problem:

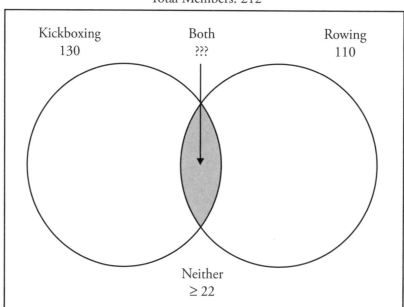

For the "Neither" category to reach ≥22, the kickboxing and rowing circles have to include no more than $212 - ≥22 = ≤190$ members. Thus since there are $130 + 110 = 240$ "memberships" in the kickboxing and rowing activities combined, there has to be an "overlap" of at least 50 members in both activities to balance the diagram out:

Total Members: 212

Thus in the scenario where exactly 50 members are involved in both kickboxing and rowing, there are 80 members involved in kickboxing only, 60 involved in rowing only, and 22 involved in neither. $50 + 80 + 60 + 22 = 212$, so the goal has been achieved.

20. **A:** If the grower produces more than twice as many 20-pound boxes as 10-pound boxes, then more than $\frac{2}{3}$ of the boxes will be 20-pound boxes. Therefore less than $\frac{1}{3}$ of the boxes will be 10-pound boxes.

Furthermore, each 20-pound box contains twice as much fruit, by weight, as does a 10-pound box. Therefore for every pound of pomegranates packaged in 10-pound boxes, more than $(2)(2) = 4$ pounds will come from 20-pound boxes. This means that less than $\frac{1}{1+(2)(2)} = \frac{1}{5}$, or 20%, of the weight of the packaged pomegranates comes from 10-pound boxes. Only Choice A is less than 20%.

For a numerical example, assume there are ten 10-pound boxes filled. Then, at least 21 20-pound boxes must be filled. Assuming these numbers, $10 \times 10 = 100$ pounds of pomegranates come from 10-pound boxes, and $21 \times 20 = 420$ pounds come from 20-pound boxes. Thus, only $\frac{100}{100+420} = \frac{100}{520} \approx 19.23\%$ of the weight of pomegranates comes from 10-pound boxes.

Word Problems: Hard Practice Question Solutions

1. A: In this problem, we have two unknowns: the number of five inch pieces and the number of seven inch pieces. However, we only have one equation to relate them, namely, that the total length of the various pieces must equal 135 inches. In general such a problem should be unsolvable, but there is a _hidden constraint_: that the number of pieces must be integers, with no remaining steel left over. Thus there is a solution (in fact, multiple solutions), and since the question asks for the minimum number of five inch steel pieces, we can find that single solution.

Note that a "trade" is possible between 7 five inch pieces and 5 seven inch pieces; they each equal 35 inches. We can start the solution process by noting that it is possible to make up 135 inches by using 27 five inch pieces and no seven inch pieces. Afterwards, we can keep trading 7 five inch pieces for 5 seven inch pieces in order to generate further solutions. The table below shows the possibilities:

Number of five inch pieces	Number of seven inch pieces
27	0
20	5
13	10
6	15

Because a further trade is impossible (we cannot have a negative number of five inch pieces), the minimum possible number of five inch pieces is 6. **Quantity A is greater.**

2. B: The probability that the first two socks will be brown is $\dfrac{6}{10} \times \dfrac{5}{9} = \dfrac{30}{90}$, whereas the probability that the first two socks will be black is $\dfrac{4}{10} \times \dfrac{3}{9} = \dfrac{12}{90}$. (These calculations reflect the Domino Effect of probability problems without replacement, in which the probability of an event is affected by a previous event—namely, the previous sock being removed from the drawer.)

The total probability of matching socks is given by $\dfrac{6}{10} \times \dfrac{5}{9} + \dfrac{4}{10} \times \dfrac{3}{9} = \dfrac{42}{90} = \dfrac{7}{15}$.

3. A: This problem is well-suited to the "$1 - x$" Shortcut. We can calculate the probability of each of the four rolls resulting in a _different_ number each time as follows: The first roll is assigned a probability of 1, since the first number that comes up will not be the same as that of any previous roll (because there has been no previous roll). In the next roll, the first number that came up must be excluded, so that there are 5 allowable outcomes. Likewise, the third roll will have 4 allowable outcomes, and the fourth roll will have 3 allowable outcomes. The overall probability of all four numbers being distinct is therefore equal to $1 \times \dfrac{5}{6} \times \dfrac{4}{6} \times \dfrac{3}{6} = 1 \times \dfrac{5}{6} \times \dfrac{\cancel{4}}{3} \times \dfrac{1}{\cancel{2}} = \dfrac{5}{18}$. Thus, the probability of at least two rolls resulting in the same number is $1 - \dfrac{5}{18} = \dfrac{13}{18}$. We can determine that this number is greater than 70% (or 0.7) by using the GRE onscreen Calculator: $\dfrac{13}{18} = 0.7222\overline{2}$.

4. 45: In order to solve this multi-part ratio problem, we must first establish a Common Term. As given, the number of managers appears as 3 in one ratio and as 5 in the other. The least common multiple of 3 and 5 is 15. Thus, by multiplying the first ratio by 5 and the second ratio by 3, we can make the number of managers the same, enabling us to combine the two ratios into one:

$$W : M = 20 : 3 = 100 : 15 \text{ and } M : D = 5 : 1 = 15 : 3, \text{ so that } W : M : D = 100 : 15 : 3.$$

So, for every 3 directors, there will be 15 managers and 100 workers. Thus a "unit" of employees is $3 + 15 + 100 = 118$. From this, we see that the total number of employees will need to be some integer multiple of 118. The only such number between 300 and 400 is $3 \times 118 = 354$. Thus, the number of managers will be given by the same multiplier: $3 \times 15 = 45$.

5. 7: The median value of the 6 integers other than x is the average of the two middle terms: $\dfrac{5+7}{2} = 6$. If x is 5 or less, the median of the set of 7 numbers will be 5. If x is 7 or greater, the median of the 7 numbers will be 7. Finally, if x is 6, then the median of the 7 numbers will be 6.

Thus let us test these cases:

Value of x	Current median of the whole set	Median if x decreases by 1	Median if x increases by 1
5	5	5	6
6	6	5	7
7	7	6	7

From these observations, we can see that the only way for the median to stay _unchanged_ when x increases, but to _decrease by 1_ when x decreases, is for x to equal 7. (Note that if x is 4 or less, or 8 or more, the median will not change at all when x increases or decreases by 1.)

6. 3.5: Sally's rate of work is half of Jane's rate of 40 pancakes per minute, and is thus 20 pancakes per minute. Using the Work Equation $R \times t = W$, we can solve for the time that Sally flips the first 30 pancakes: $t_1 = \dfrac{W}{R} = \dfrac{30}{20} = 1\dfrac{1}{2}$ minutes. After Sally is joined by Jane, the two work at the _combined_ rate of 60 pancakes per minute, flipping the remaining 120 pancakes in $t_2 = \dfrac{W}{R} = \dfrac{120}{60} = 2$ minutes. Their total time to flip 150 pancakes is therefore equal to the sum of t_1 and t_2: $1\dfrac{1}{2} + 2 = 3\dfrac{1}{2} = 3.5$ minutes.

7. **B:** Probably the most effective way to solve this problem is to use an *RTD* chart. In setting up the chart, we will use units of miles and hours; therefore, the 40 minutes will need to be written as $\dfrac{40}{60} = \dfrac{2}{3}$ hours to be consistent. Let us define t as the time, in hours, that Jake spends riding his bike. In that case, he must spend $\dfrac{2}{3} - t$ hours walking.

The *RTD* chart then is:

Travel	R (miles/hour)	T (hours)	D (miles)
Bike	10	t	$10t$
Walk	3	$\dfrac{2}{3} - t$	$3\left(\dfrac{2}{3} - t\right) = 2 - 3t$
Total	*N/A*	$\dfrac{2}{3}$	$(10t) + (2 - 3t) = 7t + 2$

In order to solve for t, we need to use the fact that Jake travels $\dfrac{2}{3}$ of the distance on his bike and $\dfrac{1}{3}$ of the distance on foot. Thus, the distance he travels on his bike is two times the distance he travels on foot: $10t = 2(2 - 3t) = 4 - 6t$, such that $16t = 4$ and $t = \dfrac{1}{4}$ hour. The total distance that Jake travels is then $7t + 2 = 7\left(\dfrac{1}{4}\right) + 2 = \dfrac{15}{4}$ miles.

(Note that this chart could also be set up with t as the column solved for, and d as the variable.)

8. **60:** There are a two primary ways to approach this problem (each with its own intuitive appeal). Before solving the problem, note that if order did not matter at all, John could choose a total of 5 committees. The formula for (5 Choose 4) is $\dfrac{5!}{4! \times 1!} = 5$. If, on the other hand, order always mattered, John could choose a total of 120 committees: $\dfrac{5!}{1!} = 120$.

We cannot use either formula here since order matters with respect to some of the selections, but not for others. To see this, think of John drawing names out of a hat, assigning President to the first name chosen, Vice President to second name chosen, and Treasurer to the third and fourth names chosen. Notice that the order of the first two selections matters (as it determines which person is the President and which person is the Vice President), but does _not_ matter for the next two selections (picking a certain person as the first Treasurer is the same as choosing him or her as the second Treasurer). Based on this, we know that the number of committees should be greater than 5 but less than 120.

Solution method 1: There are 5 ways to choose a President from among the 5 candidates. Once a President has been chosen, there are 4 ways to choose a Vice President (since there are only 4 candidates remaining after the President has been selected). There are then 3 committee members remaining from which to choose, and order does not matter. Thus there are (3 Choose 2) = $\dfrac{3!}{2! \times 1!}$ = 3 ways to choose 2 Treasurers. Therefore the answer is $5 \times 4 \times 3 = 60$.

<u>Solution method 2</u>: There are (5 Choose 4) = $\dfrac{5!}{4! \times 1!}$ = 5 ways to choose 4 people from among a group of 5. Suppose we've chosen 4 people and we've assigned them the following posts: *VP, T, P,* and *T*. We then ask how many ways we could have assigned the positions once we chose those 4 people, i.e., how many ways can we arrange the titles *VP, T, P,* and *T*? Using the Anagram Method, there are $\dfrac{4!}{2! \times 1! \times 1!}$ = 12 ways to arrange these titles. Thus there are 5 groups of people with 12 arrangements of titles. Using the Fundamental Counting Principle, $5 \times 12 = 60$ different possible committees.

9. **E:** First, notice that 4 attendees will not donate $1,200, as each person would donate only $220 ($300 minus $20 for each attendee) for a total of $880. If 5 guests attend, each will donate $200, for a total of $1,000. If 6 guests attend, each will donate $180, for a total of $1,080. If 7 guests attend, each will donate $160, for a total of $1,120. If 8 guests attend, each will donate $140, for a total of $1,120. In table form:

Number of Guests Attending Event	Donation per Attendee	Total Contribution
4	$220	$880
5	$200	$1,000
6	$180	$1,080
7	$160	<u>$1,120</u>
8	$140	<u>$1,120</u>
9	$120	$1,080

As can be seen, beyond 8 attendees, the per-attendee donation is falling faster than the number of attendees is rising, so the total contribution is falling. Thus, the maximum that can be raised at this fundraiser is $1,120, which is not enough money to build the park. The correct answer is E.

10. **B:** We want to minimize *trippim*, so we should maximize the other coins, beginning with the *megam* because we want to keep the number of coins low. Divide $3.21 by 19 cents and find the remainder. $\dfrac{\$3.21}{\$0.19} = 16$, with a remainder of 17 (i.e., $16\dfrac{17}{19}$). Since 17 is an odd number, we must have one *trippim* and therefore three *duom*, making 20 coins exactly.

It can be shown, incidentally, that no other combination of coins can exist such that the man has 20 coins or fewer.

11. **C:** Given the information about the fraction of boys who are shorter than the shortest girl and the fraction of girls who are taller than the tallest boy, the number of boys in the class must be a multiple of 5 while the number of girls must be a multiple of 3 (since the number of boys and girls must take on integer values).

The only combination of a multiple of 5 and multiple of 3 that sum to 16 is $2 \times 5 = 10$ boys and $2 \times 3 = 6$ girls. Of the 10 boys, 2 are shorter than the shortest girl. Of the 6 girls, 2 are taller than the tallest boy. Therefore, the order of heights must be as follows:

B, B, G, _, _, _, _, _, _, _, _, *B, G, G*

This implies that there must be exactly 10 students that are taller than the shortest girl and shorter than the tallest

boy. This equals $\dfrac{10}{16} = \dfrac{5}{8} = 62.5\%$.

12. $\dfrac{12}{77}$ **(Or any fractional equivalent):** In order to find the range of the set, we must first determine the largest and

smallest members of the set. We can compare the fractions in pairs to determine which is the larger in each pair. Note that, to quickly compare two fractions, we can cross-multiply the numerators and denominators and write the results next to the numerators. Whichever product is greater will indicate which fraction is greater.

For example, comparing $\dfrac{2}{3}$ to $\dfrac{8}{11}$, we cross-multiply. This comparison is the same as comparing to 2×11 to 8×3 : $22 < 24$, so $\dfrac{2}{3} < \dfrac{8}{11}$.

Proceeding likewise, we can determine that $\dfrac{8}{11}$ is, in fact, the largest of all the fractions, whereas $\dfrac{4}{7}$ is the smallest.

The range of the set is the difference between the largest and the smallest members:

$$\frac{8}{11} - \frac{4}{7} = \frac{8 \times 7 - 4 \times 11}{77} = \frac{56 - 44}{77} = \frac{12}{77}.$$

13. $\dfrac{16}{5}$ **(Or any fractional equivalent):** The given facts can be written as $30O = 12D$ and $5M = 20O$. We need to

relate muxes to darbles, so we need to eliminate oobers from the system of equations. This will be simpler if the same multiple of oobers appears in each equation. The least common multiple of 30 and 20 is 60, so let us therefore multiply the first equation by 2 and the second equation by 3:

$$60O = 24D \text{ and } 15M = 60O$$

Equating, we obtain $24D = 15M$.

We can turn this equation into the ratio of muxes to darbles by dividing by 15 and by D: $\dfrac{M}{D} = \dfrac{24}{15} = \dfrac{8}{5}$. The ratio of

two muxes to one darble is twice that, or $\dfrac{16}{5}$. (Note that it is not necessary to fully reduce fractions in order to get

credit for a right answer; fractions such as $\dfrac{32}{10}$ or $\dfrac{48}{15}$ are also considered correct.)

14. **B, D,** and **F:** We can use the Anagram Method to determine the number of possible ways to award the three medals. Let G, S and B represent the medalists and N represent non-medalists (if any). Also, we can use numbers to designate the participants. If there are three participants, the Anagram Grid looks like this:

1	2	3
G	S	B

The total number of ways to award the medals in this case is $3! = 6$. If there are four participants, the grid looks like:

1	2	3	4
G	S	B	N

In this case the total number of possibilities equals $4! = 24$. Lastly, when there are five participants, the grid looks like:

1	2	3	4	5
G	S	B	N	N

Here we have a repeated letter N; thus the number of possible anagrams is found as $\dfrac{5!}{2!} = \dfrac{120}{2} = 60$.

15. **35:** We can express the given relationships as $S = C + \dfrac{1}{4}C = \dfrac{5}{4}C$ and $C = T - \dfrac{2}{5}T = \dfrac{3}{5}T$. We can reverse the latter to yield $T = \dfrac{5}{3}C$. We can now use the Hidden Constraint in the problem: the number of each item of clothing has to be an integer. Thus, the number C of cardigans has to be divisible both by 4 (to yield an integer number of sweaters) and by 3 (to yield an integer number of turtlenecks). The smallest number is 12, which is the least common multiple of 4 and 3. With $C = 12$, we can obtain $S = 15$ and $T = 20$, so at minimum, $S + T = 35$.

16. **B** and **D:** Choice A is incorrect because 2 standard deviations above the mean is at approximately the 98th percentile, or 48 percentile points away from the mean. By contrast, Charlie's score was 45 percentile points away from the mean since the distribution is approximately normal, and thus it is also approximately symmetric.

Choice B is correct. If Joe's score places him at approximately the 98th percentile and Charlie's score was at the 5th percentile, then about 93 percent of the class scored between Joe and Charlie: 93% of 500 = 465. (For the same reason, Choice C is incorrect.)

Choice D is the toughest to evaluate. By definition, each percentile encompasses 5 scores (when the scores are ranked from lowest to highest). The percentile is defined as the score that separates the highest score in the preceding percentile from the lowest score in the next percentile. Thus for example, in a class of 500, the 1st percentile score would be defined as the average of the 5th lowest and 6th lowest scores. Similarly, Charlie's score equals the average of the 25th and 26th lowest scores on the test. Those two values have to be equal, because Charlie's score had to be an integer and had to be equal in value to either the 25th or 26th highest score. Thus at least one other student received exactly the same score as Charlie.

To use a numerical example, say the 25th lowest score was a 30 and the 26th lowest score was a 31. Then the 5th percentile would be defined as 30.5—an impossible score to obtain, because all scores were given on an integer scale between 0–100. If the 25th lowest score was a 30 and the 26th lowest score was a 32, then Charlie would have had to score a 31, which would put him in between the 25th and 26th lowest scores. This too is impossible, because then

Charlie would not have scored the 25th or 26th lowest score—and he has to have a score equal to <u>one</u> of them! Thus, to put it succinctly, Charlie's score <u>had</u> to match that of the 25th lowest and the 26th lowest scores, making them equal, and meaning that <u>at least</u> one other student received the same score Charlie received.

17. **C:** The key to answering this question is to be able to calculate the probability of rolling exactly 0, 1, 2, 3, and 4 strikes in the 4 frames he rolls.

The easiest probability to calculate is the probability of rolling a strike 4 times in a row. Let us denote that as P(*SSSS*), i.e., the probability of 4 strikes (*S*) in a row. By the "AND" principle, we should multiply the probability of rolling a strike 4 times: $(40\%)(40\%)(40\%)(40\%) = 0.4^4 = 0.0256$, or 2.56%. Thus Choice A is incorrect—

Tom's probability of rolling 4 strikes in a row is less than 3%.

Next easiest is to calculate the probability of 4 non-strikes in a row. Let us denote that as P(*NNNN*), i.e., the probability of 4 non-strikes (*N*) in a row. By the "1 – *x*" principle, the probability of a non-strike is 1 – 40% = 60%. By the "AND" principle, we should multiply the probability of rolling a non-strike 4 times: $(60\%)(60\%)(60\%)(60\%) = 0.6^4 = 0.1296$, or 12.96%. Thus Choice B is incorrect—Tom's probability of rolling no strikes at all is greater than 10%.

Calculating 1, 2, or 3 strikes is more difficult. Let's evaluate one scenario: Tom rolls a strike in the first frame, and then non-strikes in the subsequent frames. The probability of this is P(*SNNN*) = $(40\%)(60\%)(60\%)(60\%) = 0.4^1 \times 0.6^3 = 0.0864$. However, Tom can get exactly 1 strike in 4 different ways: (1) get a strike on frame 1, (2) get a strike on frame 2, (3) get a strike on frame 3, or (4) get a strike on frame 4. Since these probabilities are all equal, we can simply take $4 \times 0.0864 = 0.3456 = 34.56\%$. This is the probability of getting exactly 1 strike on any of the frames.

Incidentally, we can now disprove Choice D. Since Tom will get no strikes 12.96% of the time and 1 strike 34.56% of the time, he will get 2 or more strikes 100% – 12.96% – 34.56% = 52.48% of the time.

To calculate 2 strikes, we follow similar logic. The probability of (*SSNN*), strikes on the first two frames only, is $(40\%)(40\%)(60\%)(60\%) = 0.4^2 \times 0.6^2 = 0.0576$. However, *SSNN* is an anagram, and there are thus $\dfrac{4!}{2! \times 2!} = 6$ different ways to get exactly two strikes. The odds of exactly 2 strikes are thus $6 \times 0.0576 = 0.3456 = 34.56\%$.

This is <u>*exactly*</u> equal to the odds of rolling 1 strike, so Choice C is correct.

Incidentally, the odds of rolling exactly 3 strikes, following the same logic, is $4 \times$ P(*SSSN*) =

$4 \times (40\%)(40\%)(40\%)(60\%) = 4 \times 0.4^3 \times 0.6^1 = 15.36\%$.

18. **A:** If it takes the hot water hose h minutes to fill the hot tub, then it fills $\frac{1}{h}$ of the hot tub per minute. Similarly, if it takes the cold water hose c minutes to fill the hot tub, then it fills $\frac{1}{c}$ of the hot tub per minute. Working combined, they fill $\frac{1}{h} + \frac{1}{c} = \frac{c+h}{hc}$ of the hot tub per minute. In other words, it will take $\frac{hc}{c+h}$ minutes to fill the hot tub.

Therefore the comparison becomes:

$$\frac{h^2}{c+h} \qquad\qquad\qquad\qquad \frac{hc}{c+h}$$

Since $c < h$ and both c and h must be positive, **Quantity A is greater.**

19. **E:** The parts of the Venn diagram corresponding to this description are as follows:

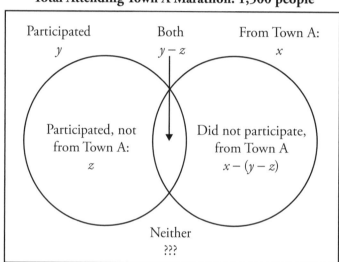

Total Attending Town A Marathon: 1,500 people

Thus we need to subtract the values inside the circles from 1,500 to arrive at the number of individuals who neither are from Town A nor participated in the marathon. This is equal to $x + y$, minus the overlap region, which is $(y - z)$. The quantity inside the circles is thus $[y + x - (y - z)]$. The correct answer is therefore $1,500 - [y + x - (y - z)] = 1500 - y - x + y - z = 1,500 - x - z$. Choice E is correct.

20. **B:** The easiest way to calculate this problem is to think in terms of the Slot Method. Each of the 3 digits can be filled by one of 9 numbers; each of 3 slots has thus 9 different options. By the Fundamental Counting Principle, we multiply the number of options for each choice to solve for the total number of possible choices: $9 \times 9 \times 9 = 729$.

However, this will erroneously include the scenarios where all 3 digits are the same. We need to subtract those possibilities out. To determine how many such options there are, we need to again consider the Slot Method. There are 9 possible values (each of the digits 1-9) that will satisfy the constraint that all 3 digits are the same. However, once that slot has been filled, each of the remaining slots now only has one choice: the same digit that was selected for the first slot. Thus there are $9 \times 1 \times 1 = 9$ possible 3-digit integers where all 3 digits are the same.

Subtracting these 9 integers out, we get a result of $729 - 9 = 720$ integers that fit the question. Choice B is the correct answer.

Considering grad school?
Get ready with *Manhattan* GRE.

Manhattan GMAT's high-quality test preparation and top-notch teaching are now available for the GRE.

How we are different:

Excellent Teachers

Manhattan GRE hires fewer than 1 in 10 qualified applicants, and instructors make 4 times the industry average. We invest in the best—you learn from the best.

Focused, In-Depth Materials

Our course materials break the GRE down subject-by-subject, allowing us to cover specific content areas more thoroughly. Rather than relying on an all-in-one guide, take charge of your GRE prep and focus on the topics that need the most work.

Great Online Resources

Unlike tests you've taken before, the GRE is computer adaptive. This unfamiliar format often confuses test-takers, resulting in lower scores. Manhattan GRE offers access to 6 full-length online practice exams.

Updated for the 2011 GRE

Our full curriculum and study materials have been updated to reflect the changes in the new GRE.

Manhattan GRE
A New Standard in GRE Prep

For more about our GRE materials and course offerings,
visit www.manhattangre.com or call us at (212) 721-7400.

mbaMission

Every candidate has a unique story to tell.

We have the creative experience to help you tell yours.

We are **mbaMission**, published authors with elite MBA experience who will work with you one-on-one to craft complete applications that will force the admissions committees to take notice. Benefit from straightforward guidance and personal mentorship as you define your unique attributes and reveal them to the admissions committees via a story only you can tell.

We will guide you through our "Complete Start to Finish Process":

- ☑ Candidate assessment, application strategy and program selection
- ☑ Brainstorming and selection of essay topics
- ☑ Outlining and essay structuring
- ☑ Unlimited essay editing
- ☑ Letter of recommendation advice
- ☑ Resume construction and review
- ☑ Interview preparation, mock interviews and feedback
- ☑ Post-acceptance and scholarship counseling

Monday Morning Essay Tip: Overrepresenting Your Overrepresentation

Many in the MBA application pool—particularly male investment bankers—worry that they are overrepresented. While you cannot change your work history, you can change the way you introduce yourself to admissions committees. Consider the following examples:

Example 1: "As an investment banking analyst at Bank of America, I am responsible for creating Excel models...."
Example 2: "At 5:30 pm, I could rest easy. The deadline for all other offers had passed. At that point, I knew...."

In the first example, the candidate starts off by mistakenly introducing the reader to the very over-representation that he/she should be trying to avoid emphasizing. In the second example, the banker immerses the reader in an unraveling mystery. This keeps the reader intrigued and focused on the applicant's story and actions rather than making the specific job title and responsibilities the center of the text. While each applicant's personal situation is different, every candidate can approach his/her story so as to mitigate the effects of overrepresentation.

To schedule a free consultation and read more than fifty Monday Morning Essay Tips, please visit our website:
www.mbamission.com

L *Manhattan* LSAT
Different Exam,
Same Standard of Excellence

From the teachers who created Manhattan GMAT, the Manhattan LSAT Strategy Guides deliver the same standard of excellence to students studying for the LSAT.

Every Guide uses real LSAT questions and delves deeply into one particular section of the LSAT exam. Together, the Strategy Guides form the heart of our advanced, flexible curriculum, featuring techniques developed to train students to think like a top scorer.

SAVE 10%
When you buy a Guide from
ManhattanLSAT.com. Use code:
MGMAT10GUIDE

Focus and Breadth:

Manhattan LSAT Guides can be stand-alone courses-in-a book, going far beyond a simple textbook.

Written by the Best:

The Manhattan LSAT Guides and curriculum were developed by master teachers with 99th percentile scores.

Online Resources:

Access to a Proctor LSAT Video, study syllabus, a 3-hour LSAT Class, and more.

Student Testimonials

"The [Strategy Guides] were extremely helpful. Providing many different examples and different methods of approaching problems made the curricular materials an amazing help." – Manhattan LSAT Online Student, 2009

"The Strategy Guides were excellent, so much better than any other books I've used. I liked that the material was so concise and allowed you to practice questions in detail." – Manhattan LSAT Online Student, 2009

Finally, a GMAT® prep guide series that goes beyond the basics.

Number Properties, Fourth Edition
ISBN: 978-0-9824238-4-4
Retail: $26

Fractions, Decimals, & Percents, Fourth Edition
ISBN: 978-0-9824238-2-0
Retail: $26

Equations, Inequalities, & VICs, Fourth Edition
ISBN: 978-0-9824238-1-3
Retail: $26

Word Translations, Fourth Edition
ISBN: 978-0-9824238-7-5
Retail: $26

Geometry, Fourth Edition
ISBN: 978-0-9824238-3-7
Retail: $26

Critical Reasoning, Fourth Edition
ISBN: 978-0-9824238-0-6
Retail: $26

Reading Comprehension, Fourth Edition
ISBN: 978-0-9824238-5-1
Retail: $26

Sentence Correction, Fourth Edition
ISBN: 978-0-9824238-6-8
Retail: $26

Published by

Manhattan GMAT

 You get many more pages per topic than you find in all-in-one tomes.

 Only buy those guides that address the specific skills you need to develop.

 Gain access to Online Practice GMAT Exams & Bonus Question Banks.

COMMENTS FROM GMAT TEST TAKERS:

Now Available at your local bookstore!

"Bravo, Manhattan GMAT! Bravo! The guides truly did not disappoint. All the guides are clear, concise, and well organized, and explained things in a manner that made it possible to understand things the first time through without missing any of the important details."

"I've thumbed through a lot of books that don't even touch these. The fact that they're split up into components is immeasurably helpful. The set-up of each guide and the lists of past GMAT problems make for an incredibly thorough and easy-to-follow study path."

GMAT and GMAC are registered trademarks of the Graduate Management Admission Council which neither sponsors nor endorses this product.